2025
BLACKSTONE
GRIDDLE
RECIPE BOOK

2000 Days of Simple, Delicious, and Flavorful Recipes Cookbook for Beginners | Your Ultimate Guide to Outdoor Grilling Game

Petijutria Krulopeger

Copyright© 2025 By Petijutria Krulopeger

All rights reserved worldwide.

No part of this book may be reproduced or transmitted in any form or by any means, electronic or mechanical, including photo- copying, recording or by any information storage and retrieval system, without written permission from the publisher, except for the inclusion of brief quotations in a review.

Warning-Disclaimer

The purpose of this book is to educate and entertain. The author or publisher does not guarantee that anyone following the techniques, suggestions, tips, ideas, or strategies will become successful. The author and publisher shall have neither liability or responsibility to anyone with respect to any loss or damage caused, or alleged to be caused, directly or indirectly by the information contained in this book.

TABLE OF CONTENTS

1	Introduction	
3	Chapter 1	Breakfasts
12	Chapter 2	Poultry
22	Chapter 3	Fish and Seafood
32	Chapter 4	Beef, Pork, and Lamb
43	Chapter 5	Pizzas, Wraps, and Sandwiches
50	Chapter 6	Vegetables and Sides
58	Chapter 7	Snacks and Appetizers
63	Chapter 8	Desserts
67	Appendix 1:	Measurement Conversion Chart
68	Appendix 2:	Recipes Index

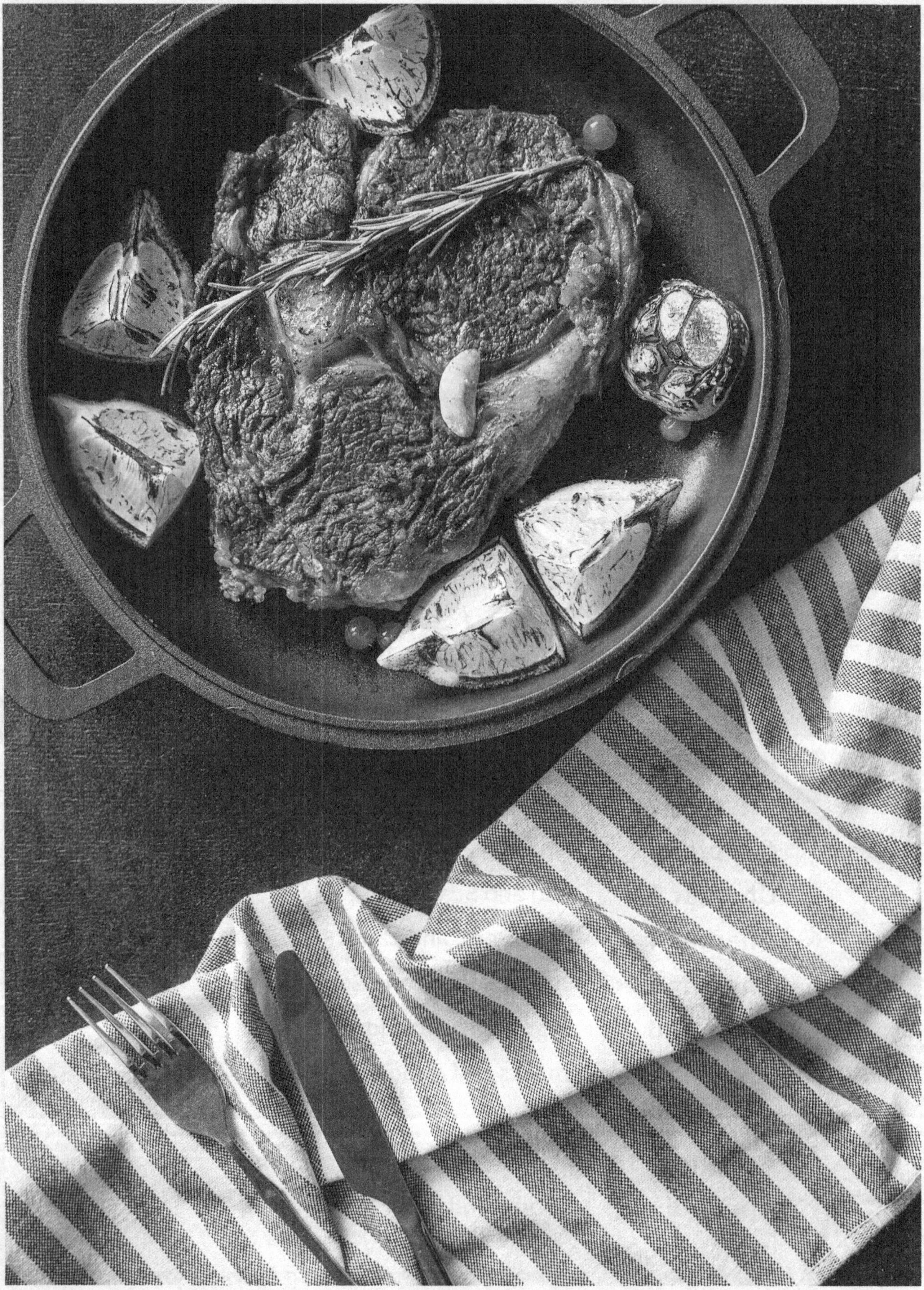

INTRODUCTION

The 2025 Blackstone Griddle Recipe Book stands as a beacon for both amateur and seasoned chefs who are looking to enhance their outdoor cooking game. This comprehensive guide is not just a collection of recipes; it's a lifestyle manual that champions simplicity, flavor, and the joy of preparing meals in the great outdoors. With over 2000 days' worth of dishes, this book is designed to introduce you to a world of culinary delights that are easy to prepare, nutritious, and sure to impress.

Embracing Healthy Eating

In today's fast-paced world, healthy eating is often a challenge. However, the 2025 Blackstone Griddle Recipe Book makes it both achievable and enjoyable. The recipes are crafted with a focus on nutrition, ensuring that each dish is a balanced meal. From grilled vegetables and lean proteins to whole-grain accompaniments, the book is a testament to the fact that healthy eating does not have to be bland or time-consuming. Each recipe is a step towards a healthier lifestyle, providing the necessary nutrients while tantalizing your taste buds.

The Art of Outdoor Cooking

Outdoor cooking has long been associated with relaxation, adventure, and a sense of accomplishment. The Blackstone Griddle Recipe Book takes this experience to a new level by offering a plethora of recipes that are perfect for grilling, searing, and roasting. Whether you are an experienced griller or a beginner, this book provides you with the knowledge and confidence to tackle any outdoor cooking challenge. The 详细的 of each recipe ensure that you can replicate these dishes with ease, allowing you to focus on the joy of cooking rather than the stress of preparation.

Mastering the Cooking Process

One of the standout features of the 2025 Blackstone Griddle Recipe Book is its focus on making outdoor cooking accessible and stress-free. Each recipe is accompanied by detailed instructions that guide you through the cooking process from start to finish. The emphasis on simple techniques and easy-to-follow steps ensures that even the most inexperienced cook can achieve delicious results. Furthermore, the book includes troubleshooting tips and advice on how to deal with common cooking issues, ensuring that your outdoor cooking experience is always a success.

A Diversity of Flavors and Cuisine

The beauty of outdoor cooking lies in its versatility, and the Blackstone Griddle Recipe Book fully embrace this concept. The book boasts a wide range of recipes that cater to different tastes and dietary preferences. From classic American dishes to international cuisine, there is something for everyone. Whether you are in the mood for a hearty barbecue, a light salad, or a gourmet meal, this book has you covered. The recipes are a blend of traditional favorites and innovative dishes, ensuring that your outdoor cooking adventures never get boring.

Conclusion

The 2025 Blackstone Griddle Recipe Book is more than just a cookbook; it's a gateway to a world of delicious and healthy outdoor cooking. With its emphasis on simple, nutritious, and flavorful recipes, this book is the perfect companion for anyone looking to enhance their cooking skills and enjoy the outdoors. Whether you are hosting a barbecue, a family picnic, or a casual get-together, the Blackstone Griddle Recipe Book will help you prepare dishes that are sure to impress and delight. So, grab your griddle, your ingredients, and get ready to embark on a culinary adventure that is both rewarding and enjoyable.

Chapter 1 Breakfasts

Chapter 1 Breakfasts

Creamy Buttermilk Pancakes

Prep time: 10 minutes | Cook time: 8 minutes | Serves 3

- 2 cups all-purpose flour
- 3 tablespoons sugar
- 2 teaspoons baking powder
- 2 teaspoons baking soda
- pinch kosher salt
- 2 eggs
- 2½ cups buttermilk
- ¼ cup melted butter

1. Sift the flour, sugar, baking powder, baking soda, and salt together in a large bowl. 2. In a medium bowl, whisk the eggs, buttermilk, and melted butter together until frothy, then pour into the dry ingredients. Mix until well combined but do not overmix. Small lumps will be fine. Let sit at room temperature for 20 to 30 minutes while your grill heats up. 3. Bring the griddle grill to medium-high heat. Oil the griddle and allow it to heat until the oil is shimmering but not smoking. 4. Pour about ¼ cup batter onto the griddle grill for each pancake. The pancakes should slowly begin to form bubbles. After 2 to 4 minutes, when the bubbles pop and leave small holes, flip the pancake. Cook for an additional 2 minutes.

Tender Ham and Swiss Delight

Prep time: 8 minutes | Cook time: 12 minutes | Serves 2

- 2 tablespoons oil
- ½ red bell pepper, thinly sliced
- 6 thin slices Black Forest ham
- 4 thin slices Swiss cheese
- 2 prepared crepes
- 2 teaspoons Dijon mustard

1. Bring the griddle grill to medium and heat the oil. Sauté the bell pepper strips for 5 to 7 minutes, until wilted. Set aside and keep warm. 2. Spread ham slices out on the griddle grill and warm them for about 5 minutes on one side. Flip the ham and arrange into two piles of three slices, letting the slices overlap. 3. Place two slices of cheese on each of the piles of ham, add a few tablespoons of water to the griddle, and cover to help the cheese melt. 4. While the cheese is melting, warm the crepes on the griddle and spread half the mustard on each. Top with the ham and melted cheese and sauteed bell peppers. Fold and serve.

Crispy Hash Brown Scramble

Prep time: 10 minutes | Cook time: 10 minutes | Serves 4

- 2 russet potatoes, shredded, rinsed, and drained
- 8 eggs, beaten
- 1 cup cheddar cheese
- 6 slices bacon, cut into small pieces
- ⅓ cup green onion, chopped
- vegetable oil

1. Preheat griddle to medium heat and brush with vegetable oil. 2. On one side, place the potatoes on the griddle and spread in a ½ inch thick layer. Cook the potatoes until golden brown and then flip. Add the bacon to the other side of the griddle and cook until the fat has rendered. 3. Add the eggs and cheese to the top of the hash browns and stir in the bacon and green onion. Cook until the cheese has melted and divide equally among 4 plates.

Golden Johnny Cakes

Prep time: 10 minutes | Cook time: 6 minutes | Serves 1

- 2 eggs
- 1⅓ cups milk
- 1 tablespoon honey
- ¼ cup cooking oil
- 1½ cups all-purpose flour
- ½ cup fine cornmeal
- 4 teaspoons baking powder
- 1 tablespoon sugar
- 1 teaspoon salt

1. Whisk the eggs, milk, honey, and oil in a medium bowl until frothy. Combine the flour, cornmeal, baking powder, sugar, and salt in a large bowl and stir to combine. 2. Add the wet ingredients to the dry ingredients and stir until well-incorporated and free of clumps. Let sit for 20 minutes while your grill heats up. 3. Bring the griddle grill to medium-high heat. Oil the griddle and allow it to heat until the oil is shimmering but not smoking. 4. Pour about ¼ cup of batter onto the griddle grill for each pancake. The pancakes should slowly begin to form bubbles. After 2 to 4 minutes, when the bubbles pop and leave small holes, flip the pancakes. Cook for an additional 2 minutes.

Savory Steak and Mushroom with Balsamic Glaze

Prep time: 10 minutes | Cook time: 20 minutes | Serves 2

- 2 tablespoons butter
- 8 cremini mushrooms, sliced
- 1 tablespoon minced garlic
- 1 teaspoon salt, plus more to taste
- 1 teaspoon pepper, plus more to taste
- Balsamic Griddle Sauce, as needed
- 6-ounce (170g) beef tenderloin fillet, cut in half lengthwise
- 2 prepared crepes
- cooking oil, as needed

1. Over medium heat, melt the butter and sauté the mushrooms with the garlic and 1 teaspoon each of salt and pepper. 2. The salt will help release the moisture from the mushrooms. When this begins, add ¾ cup of the Balsamic Griddle Sauce to the mushrooms and cover. Stir occasionally for 6 to 8 minutes, and set aside to keep warm. 3. Increase the heat on the griddle grill to medium high and while it is heating, scrape and clean any residual balsamic sauce from the cooking surface so it does not burn. 4. Pat the beef dry with paper towels, and season liberally with salt and pepper. 5. Add cooking oil to the griddle, and when it begins to shimmer, add the steak and sear for 3 minutes. Flip and sear for an additional 1 to 3 minutes, based on your desired doneness. 6. Allow the steak to rest for 10 minutes, then cut across the grain into thin slices. Arrange the steak on a crepe and top with mushrooms.

Artisanal Grilled Pizza with Eggs and Greens

Prep time: 10 minutes | Cook time: 8 minutes | Serves 2

- 2 tablespoons all-purpose flour, plus more as needed
- ½ store-bought pizza dough (about 8 ounces / 227 g)
- 1 tablespoon canola oil, divided
- 1 cup fresh ricotta cheese
- 4 large eggs
- Sea salt
- Freshly ground black pepper
- 4 cups arugula, torn
- 1 tablespoon extra-virgin olive oil
- 1 teaspoon freshly squeezed lemon juice
- 2 tablespoons grated Parmesan cheese

1. Preheat the griddle to medium high. 2. Dust a clean work surface with flour. Place the dough on the floured surface, and roll it into a 9-inch round of even thickness. Dust your rolling pin and work surface with additional flour, as needed, to ensure the dough does not stick. 3. Brush the surface of the rolled-out dough evenly with ½ tablespoon of canola oil. Flip the dough over and brush with the remaining ½ tablespoon oil. Poke the dough with a fork 5 or 6 times across its surface to prevent air pockets from forming during cooking. 4. Place the dough to the grill and cook for 4 minutes. 5. After 4 minutes, flip the dough, then spoon teaspoons of ricotta cheese across the surface of the dough, leaving a 1-inch border around the edges. 6. Crack one egg into a ramekin or small bowl. This way you can easily remove any shell that may break into the egg and keep the yolk intact. Imagine the dough is split into four quadrants. Pour one egg into each. Repeat with the remaining 3 eggs. Season the pizza with salt and pepper. 7. Continue cooking for the remaining 3 to 4 minutes, until the egg whites are firm. 8. Meanwhile, in a medium bowl, toss together the arugula, oil, and lemon juice, and season with salt and pepper. Transfer the pizza to a cutting board and let it cool. Top it with the arugula mixture, drizzle with olive oil, if desired, and sprinkle with Parmesan cheese. 9. Cut into pieces and serve.

Flavorful Chorizo Breakfast Tacos

Prep time: 10 minutes | Cook time: 10 minutes | Serves 3

- 4 eggs
- ¼ cup milk
- ½ pound (227g) chorizo
- butter, as needed
- ½ cup chopped green pepper
- ½ cup diced sweet onion
- 6 corn tortillas
- ½ cup shredded cheddar cheese
- cooking oil, as needed

1. Crack the eggs into a medium bowl and whisk with the milk until well mixed. 2. Bring the griddle grill to medium-high heat. 3. When the grill is hot, begin to cook the chorizo. As the chorizo cooks, chop it continually with a stiff spatula or metal scraper to promote even cooking and browning while it breaks into small pieces. Cover the chorizo and allow it to cook completely. 4. While the chorizo continues to cook, melt a couple of pats of butter on the griddle and sauté the pepper and onion until the peppers begin to wilt and the onions start to become translucent. Combine the chorizo and vegetables and spread them out evenly on the cooking surface. 5. If needed, add more butter to make sure the griddle is well greased before you pour the egg mixture into the chopped chorizo and veggies. Using a wide spatula or scraper, stir the egg mixture while it cooks and the eggs form curds. As the eggs solidify, scrape the eggs, chorizo and veggies aside and cover to keep warm. 6. Spread a thin coat of oil on the griddle and allow it to heat until shimmering. Place the tortillas in the oil and cook for about 2 minutes per side. 7. Uncover the chorizo mixture and add the cheese on top. Cook until the cheese melts. 8. Assemble the tacos by dividing the chorizo mixture into thirds and scooping it into a double-layered tortilla, then top with cheese.

Savory Onion, Pepper, and Mushroom Frittata

Prep time: 10 minutes | Cook time: 10 minutes | Serves 4

- 4 large eggs
- ¼ cup whole milk
- Sea salt
- Freshly ground black pepper
- ½ bell pepper, seeded and diced
- ½ onion, chopped
- 4 cremini mushrooms, sliced
- ½ cup shredded Cheddar cheese

1. Preheat the griddle to medium high. 2. In a medium bowl, whisk together the eggs and milk. Season with the salt and pepper. Add the bell pepper, onion, mushrooms, and cheese. Mix until well combined. 3. Pour the egg mixture into the Ninja Multi-Purpose Pan or baking pan, spreading evenly. 4. Place the pan directly to the grill and cook for 10 minutes, or until lightly golden.

Warm Grilled Cinnamon Toast with Berries and Whipped Cream

Prep time: 15 minutes | Cook time: 10 minutes | Serves 4

- 1 (15-ounce) can full-fat coconut milk, refrigerated overnight
- ½ tablespoon powdered sugar
- 1½ teaspoons vanilla extract, divided
- 1 cup halved strawberries
- 1 tablespoon maple syrup, plus more for garnish
- 1 tablespoon brown sugar, divided
- ¾ cup lite coconut milk
- 2 large eggs
- ½ teaspoon ground cinnamon
- 2 tablespoons unsalted butter, at room temperature
- 4 slices challah bread

1. Turn the chilled can of full-fat coconut milk upside down (do not shake the can), open the bottom, and pour out the liquid coconut water. Scoop the remaining solid coconut cream into a medium bowl. Using an electric hand mixer, whip the cream for 3 to 5 minutes, until soft peaks form. 2. Add the powdered sugar and ½ teaspoon of the vanilla to the coconut cream, and whip it again until creamy. Place the bowl in the refrigerator. 3. Preheat the griddle to medium high. While the unit is preheating, combine the strawberries with the maple syrup and toss to coat evenly. 4. Sprinkle evenly with ½ tablespoon of the brown sugar. 5. In a large shallow bowl, whisk together the lite coconut milk, eggs, the remaining 1 teaspoon of vanilla, and cinnamon. 6. Place the strawberries on the grill top. Gently press the fruit down to maximize grill marks. Grill for 4 minutes without flipping. 7. Meanwhile, butter each slice of bread on both sides. Place one slice in the egg mixture and let it soak for 1 minute. Flip the slice over and soak it for another minute. Repeat with the remaining bread slices. Sprinkle each side of the toast with the remaining ½ tablespoon of brown sugar. 8. After 4 minutes, remove the strawberries from the grill and set aside. Decrease the temperature to medium low. Place the bread on the Grill and cook for 4 to 6 minutes, until golden and caramelized. Check often to ensure desired doneness. 9. Place the toast on a plate and top with the strawberries and whipped coconut cream. 10. Drizzle with maple syrup, if desired.

Diner-Style Omelet

Prep time: 10 minutes | Cook time: 10 minutes | Serves 1

- ½ cup diced red bell pepper
- ½ cup sliced mushrooms
- ½ teaspoon garlic salt
- 2 eggs plus 2 egg yolks
- ½ cup shredded cheddar-Jack cheese blend, or 2 slices cheese
- butter, as needed
- salt and pepper, to taste
- cilantro, to serve (optional)

1. Bring the griddle grill to medium-low heat. 2. Butter a portion of your griddle grill and begin to slowly sauté the peppers and mushrooms. After about 3 minutes, give the veggies a stir and sprinkle on the garlic salt, then cover. 3. Beat the eggs in a medium bowl until quite frothy. With a large spatula, move the pepper and mushroom mixture to the side of the griddle. Melt plenty of butter over a large area on the griddle and very slowly pour the eggs onto the cooking surface. The eggs will run a bit, and if you are able to use the side of the spatula to shape them into a circle or square, they will be easier to flip later on. 4. Allow the eggs to cook slowly without much poking or prodding. After about 3 minutes, you will see the eggs start to bubble as they cook. Some portions of the omelet will be firm, and some portions will be runny and raw. Distribute the peppers and mushrooms evenly across the omelet the same way you would top a pizza, in a thin layer. When about 80 percent of the egg has solidified, add the cheese in an even layer. 5. At this point, your omelet should have very little runny or visibly raw egg remaining. With a long spatula, scrape under the omelet with a quick wrist motion to make sure the egg is released from the griddle before you attempt to finish. To fold the omelet in half, slide the spatula under the omelet until the entire width of the spatula is covered, and with a lift and twist, lift the spatula and twist your wrist so the omelet folds over and flops onto itself. 6. Cook for about another minute and serve with salt and pepper to taste. Garnish with cilantro, if desired.

Timeless Steak and Eggs

Prep time: 10 minutes | Cook time: 10 minutes | Serves 4

- 1 pound (454 g) Sirloin, cut into 4 ½-inch thick pieces
- 8 large eggs
- 3 tablespoons vegetable oil
- salt and black pepper

1. Preheat griddle to medium-high heat on one side and medium heat on the other. 2. Season the steaks with a generous amount of salt and pepper. 3. Place steaks on the medium high side and cook for 3 minutes and add the oil to the medium heat side. 4. Flip the steaks and crack the eggs onto the medium heat side of the griddle. 5. After 3 minutes remove the steaks from the griddle and allow to rest 5 minutes.Finish cooking the eggs and place two eggs and one piece of steak on each plate to serve.Season the eggs with a pinch of salt and pepper.

Delightful Toad in a Hole

Prep time: 10 minutes | Cook time: 5 minutes | Serves 4

- 4 slices white, wheat, or sourdough bread
- 4 eggs
- 2 tablespoons butter
- salt and black pepper

1. Preheat griddle to medium heat add the butter, spreading it around. 2. Cut a hole in the center of each slice of bread. 3. Place the slices of bread on the griddle and crack an egg into the holes in each slice of bread. 4. Cook until the bread begins to brown, then flip and cook until the egg whites are firm. 5. Remove from the griddle and season with salt and black pepper before serving.

Savory Bacon and Gruyere Omelet

Prep time: 5 minutes | Cook time: 15 minutes | Serves 2

- 6 eggs, beaten
- 6 strips bacon
- ¼ pound (113 g) gruyere, shredded
- 1 teaspoon black pepper
- 1 teaspoon salt
- 1 tablespoon chives, finely chopped
- vegetable oil

1. Add salt to the beaten eggs and set aside for 10 minutes. 2. Heat your griddle to medium heat and add the bacon strips.Cook until most of the fat has rendered, but bacon is still flexible.Remove the bacon from the griddle and place on paper towels. 3. Once the bacon has drained, chop into small pieces. 4. Add the eggs to the griddle in two even pools.Cook until the bottom of the eggs starts to firm up.Add the gruyere to the eggs and cook until the cheese has started to melt and the eggs are just starting to brown. 5. Add the bacon pieces and use a spatula to turn one half of the omelet onto the other half. 6. Remove from the griddle, season with pepper and chives and serve.

Hearty Potato Bacon Hash

Prep time: 30 minutes | Cook time: 3 hours | Serves 6 to 8

- 6 slices thick cut bacon
- 2 russet potatoes, cut into ½ inch chunks
- 1 yellow onion, chopped
- 1 red bell pepper, chopped
- 1 clove garlic, finely chopped
- 1 teaspoon salt
- ½ teaspoon black pepper
- 1 tablespoon Tabasco sauce

1. Set your griddle to medium heat and cook the bacon until just crispy. 2. Add the potato, onion, and bell pepper to the griddle and cook until the potato has softened.Use the large surface of the griddle to spread out the ingredients. 3. When the potato has softened, add the garlic, salt, and pepper. 4. Chop the bacon into small pieces and add it to the griddle.Stir the mixture well and add the hot sauce right before removing the hash from the griddle.Serve immediately.

Hearty Ultimate Breakfast Burrito

Prep time: 5 minutes | Cook time: 20 minutes | Serves 2

- 4 eggs
- 4 strips bacon
- 1 large russet potato, peeled and cut into small cubes
- 1 red bell pepper
- ½ yellow onion
- 1 ripe avocado, sliced
- 2 tablespoons hot sauce
- 2 large flour tortillas
- vegetable oil

1. Preheat the griddle to medium-high heat on one side and medium heat on the other side.Brush with vegetable oil and add the bacon to the medium heat side and peppers and onions to the medium-high side.When the bacon finishes cooking, place on paper towels and chop into small pieces.Add the potatoes to the bacon fat on the griddle.Cook the potatoes until softened. 2. Add the eggs to the vegetable side and cook until firm.Place the ingredients onto the tortillas and top with slices of avocado and a tablespoon of hot sauce. 3. Fold the tortillas and enjoy.

Traditional Buttermilk Pancakes

Prep time: 5 minutes | Cook time: 10 minutes | Serves 4

- 2 cups all-purpose flour
- 3 tablespoons sugar
- 1½ teaspoons baking powder
- 1½ teaspoons baking soda
- 1¼ teaspoons salt
- 2½ cups buttermilk
- 2 eggs
- 3 tablespoons unsalted butter, melted
- 2 tablespoons vegetable oil

1. In a large bowl, combine the flour, sugar, baking soda, baking powder, and salt. 2. Stir in the buttermilk, eggs, and butter, and mix until combined but not totally smooth. 3. Heat your griddle to medium heat and add a small amount of oil. Using a paper towel, spread the oil over the griddle in a very thin layer. 4. Use a ladle to pour the batter onto the griddle allowing a few inches between pancakes. 5. When the surface of the pancakes is bubbly, flip and cook a few additional minutes. Remove the pancakes from the griddle and serve immediately with butter and maple syrup.

Flaky and Light Crepes

Prep time: 10 minutes | Cook time: 10 minutes | Serves 3

- 1 cup all-purpose flour
- 1½ cups milk
- ½ cup water
- 2 eggs
- 1 teaspoon grated lemon zest
- 2 pinches salt
- 2 tablespoons melted butter, plus more as needed for the griddle

1. Place all the ingredients except the butter in a blender and blend for 30 to 45 seconds until a smooth batter forms. If necessary, scrape down the sides of the blender so all the ingredients are incorporated, and blend again. Allow the batter to rest for 30 minutes. 2. Bring the griddle grill to medium heat. Butter about a 10-inch square on the griddle grill, then pour ¼ cup of the batter in the center. 3. Spread the crepe batter into a circle with the measuring cup or use a crepe spreader to create a thin, round layer on the griddle. Cook for about 90 seconds or until most of the batter has set. Flip and cook for another 60 to 90 seconds until it is between yellow and golden brown in color. (You can cook the crepes to your desired doneness, but I find cooking them to a yellowish color leaning toward golden brown is best for rolling and stuffing.)

Crispy Potato Pancakes

Prep time: 10 minutes | Cook time: 8 minutes | Serves 3

- 2 eggs
- ¼ cup milk
- 1½ cups russet potato, peeled and shredded
- ¼ cup all-purpose flour
- ¼ cup finely diced onion
- ¼ cup finely chopped green onion
- 1 teaspoon baking powder
- 1 teaspoon salt
- 1 teaspoon pepper
- cooking oil, as needed

1. In a large bowl, beat the eggs and milk until frothy. Add the remaining ingredients and stir to combine. The batter should be moist throughout but not pooling with liquid. Allow to rest for 20 minutes while the grill heats up. 2. Bring the griddle grill to medium-high heat. 3. Add a thin coat of oil to the cooking surface, and when it begins to shimmer, add about ¼ cup of potato pancake batter to the griddle for each pancake. Press the batter to flatten and cook each side for 3 to 4 minutes until golden brown.

Crispy Fried Pickles

Prep time: 10 minutes | Cook time: 10 minutes | Serves 4

- 20 dill pickle slices
- ¼ cup all-purpose flour
- ⅛ teaspoon baking powder
- 3 tablespoons beer or seltzer water
- ⅛ teaspoon sea salt
- 2 tablespoons water, plus more if needed
- 2 tablespoons cornstarch
- 1½ cups panko bread crumbs
- 1 teaspoon paprika
- 1 teaspoon garlic powder
- ¼ teaspoon cayenne pepper
- 2 tablespoons canola oil, divided

1. Preheat the griddle to medium-high. 2. Pat the pickle slices dry, and place them on a dry plate in the freezer. 3. In a medium bowl, stir together the flour, baking powder, beer, salt, and water. The batter should be the consistency of cake batter. If it is too thick, add more water, 1 teaspoon at a time. 4. Place the cornstarch in a small shallow bowl. 5. In a separate large shallow bowl, combine the bread crumbs, paprika, garlic powder, and cayenne pepper. 6. Remove the pickles from the freezer. Dredge each one in cornstarch. 7. Tap off any excess, then coat in the batter. Lastly, coat evenly with the bread crumb mixture. 8. Set on the griddle top and gently brush the breaded pickles with 1 tablespoon of oil. Cook for 5 minutes. 9. After 5 minutes, turn and gently brush the pickles with the remaining 1 tablespoon of oil and resume cooking. 10. When cooking is complete, serve immediately.

Timeless Classic French Toast

Prep time: 5 minutes | Cook time: 10 minutes | Serves 4

- 6 eggs, beaten
- ¼ cup "half and half" or heavy cream
- 8 slices thick cut white or sourdough bread
- 2 tablespoons sugar
- 1 tablespoon cinnamon
- 1 teaspoon salt - butter
- powdered sugar
- maple syrup

1. Heat your griddle to medium heat. 2. In a large bowl, combine the eggs, cream, sugar, cinnamon, and salt. Mix well until smooth. 3. Lightly grease the griddle with butter or vegetable oil. 4. Dip each slice of bread in the mixture until well saturated with egg then place onto the griddle. 5. When the French toast has begun to brown, flip and cook until the other side has browned as well. About four minutes. Remove the French toast from the griddle, dust with powdered sugar, and serve with warm maple syrup.

Elegant Eggs Belledict

Prep time: 10 minutes | Cook time: 15 minutes | Serves 2

- 1 medium red or green bell pepper
- 2 English muffins
- 2 eggs
- 4 slices Canadian bacon
- ½ cup very finely shredded Jarlsberg cheese
- butter, as needed

1. Bring the griddle grill to medium heat. Cut the uneven bottom off the bell pepper, then cut two rings of pepper about ½ inch thick. 2. Coat the griddle with a good amount of butter. Separate the English muffins and place the uncut-sides on the griddle to begin warming. Place the bell pepper rings on the griddle and cook for 2 minutes. Flip the peppers, then flip the English muffins to heat the other sides. 3. Crack an egg and carefully drop it into one of the bell pepper rings. Scoot the other pepper ring close by and repeat with the second egg. Using a cover that's just bigger than the peppers, cover the eggs and allow them to cook for 1 minute. 4. While the eggs are cooking, warm the Canadian bacon on the grilling surface. 5. Remove the cover from the eggs and squirt water around the grilling surface very close to the eggs, and immediately cover the eggs again to capture the steam and assist with cooking the whites and yolks. Cook for another minute, then cover each of the eggs with half of the cheese. The finer the cheese is grated, the more quickly it will melt, so I use a very fine grater or even a Microplane. Squirt the perimeter of the eggs again and cover to catch the steam, allowing the cheese to melt. 6. Remove the English muffins from the griddle and put 2 slices of Canadian bacon on top of each. Uncover the eggs, and using a spatula, remove the pepper ring containing the egg and slide it onto the Canadian bacon. Top with the other half of the English muffin.

Cool and Creamy Ice Cream French Toast

Prep time: 8 minutes | Cook time: 5 minutes | Serves 4

- 1 cup melted vanilla ice cream
- 3 eggs
- 1 teaspoon vanilla extract
- pinch of ground cinnamon
- 8 slices Texas toast or other thick-cut bread
- cooking oil, as needed

1. Combine the melted ice cream, eggs, vanilla extract, and cinnamon in a bowl wide enough for the bread to be easily dipped into. Mix very well or until frothy. 2. Bring the griddle grill to medium-high heat and coat the surface with oil. When the oil begins to shimmer, dip each side of the bread into the egg batter so it lightly coats each side. Allow any additional batter to drain back into the bowl. 3. Place the bread on the griddle. Cook for 3 to 4 minutes per side, or until the French toast is golden brown. Repeat with the remaining ingredients.

Tender Chicken Bacon Artichoke Delight

Prep time: 10 minutes | Cook time: 15 minutes | Serves 2

- 4 slices bacon
- 8 ounces (227g) chicken breast, cut into small cubes
- White Wine Griddle Sauce
- 3 marinated artichoke hearts, quartered
- 2 prepared crepes
- ⅓ cup ranch dressing
- salt and pepper, to taste

1. Bring the griddle grill to medium-high heat and cook the bacon. Remove and keep warm. 2. In the bacon fat, sauté the cubed chicken with salt and pepper for 4 minutes, with very little movement, allowing the chicken to brown. Add the White Wine Griddle Sauce as needed and cover to finish cooking an additional 4 to 6 minutes, or until the chicken is done. Remove and keep warm. 3. Sauté the marinated artichokes in the residual bits of cooked chicken on the griddle grill for 3 to 5 minutes until warm and slightly brown. 4. Spread about half of the ranch dressing on each crepe. Fill the crepes with chicken, bacon, and artichoke pieces.

Spicy Mexican Scramble

Prep time: 5 minutes | Cook time: 10 minutes | Serves 4

- 8 eggs, beaten
- 1 pound (454 g) Chorizo
- ½ yellow onion
- 1 cup cooked black beans
- ½ cup green chilies
- ½ cup jack cheese
- ¼ cup green onion, chopped
- ½ teaspoon black pepper
- vegetable oil

1. Preheat a griddle to medium heat. Brush the griddle with vegetable oil and add the chorizo to one side and the onions to the other side. When the onion has softened, combine it with the chorizo and add the beans and chilies. Add the eggs, cheese, and green onion and cook until eggs have reached desired firmness. 2. Remove the scramble from the griddle and season with black pepper before serving.

Hearty Sausage and Vegetable Scramble

Prep time: 10 minutes | Cook time: 20 minutes | Serves 4

- 8 eggs, beaten
- ½ pound (227 g) sausage, sliced into thin rounds or chopped
- 1 green bell pepper, sliced
- 1 yellow onion, sliced
- 1 cup white mushrooms, sliced
- 1 teaspoon salt
- ½ teaspoon black pepper
- vegetable oil

1. Preheat the griddle to medium-high heat. 2. Brush the griddle with vegetable oil and add the peppers and mushrooms. 3. Cook until lightly browned and then add the onions. Season with salt and pepper and cook until the onions are soft. 4. Add the sausage to the griddle and mix with the vegetables. Cook until lightly browned. 5. Add the eggs and mix with the vegetables and cook until eggs reach desired doneness. Use a large spatula to remove the scramble from the griddle and serve immediately.

Decadent Bacon Egg and Cheese Sandwich

Prep time: 5 minutes | Cook time: 10 minutes | Serves 4

- 4 large eggs
- 8 strips of bacon
- 4 slices cheddar or American cheese
- 8 slices sourdough bread
- 2 tablespoons butter
- 2 tablespoons vegetable oil

1. Heat your griddle to medium heat and place the strips of bacon on one side. Cook until just slightly crispy. 2. When the bacon is nearly finished, place the oil on the other side of the griddle and crack with eggs onto the griddle. Cook them either sunny side up or over medium. 3. Butter one side of each slice of bread and place them butter side down on the griddle. Place a slice of cheese on 4 of the slices of bread and when the cheese has just started to melt and the eggs are finished, stack the eggs on the bread. 4. Add the bacon to the sandwiches and place the other slice of bread on top. Serve immediately.

Uncomplicated French Crepes

Prep time: 1hour | Cook time: 15 minutes | Serves 4

- 1¼ cups flour
- ¾ cup whole milk
- ½ cup water
- 2 eggs
- 3 tablespoons unsalted butter, melted
- 1 teaspoon vanilla
- 2 tablespoons sugar

1. In a large bowl, add all the ingredients and mix with a whisk. Make sure the batter is smooth. Rest for 1 hour. 2. Heat your Blackstone Griddle to medium heat and add a thin layer of butter. Add about ¼ cup of the batter. Using a crepe spreading tool, form your crepe and cook for 1-2 minutes. Use your Crepe Spatula and flip. Cook for another minute. 3. Top with Nutella and strawberries for a sweet crepe, or top with scrambled eggs and black forest ham for a savory crepe.

Radiant Golden Hash Browns

Prep time: 10 minutes | Cook time: 15 minutes | Serves 4

- 3 russet potatoes, peeled
- 1 tablespoon onion powder
- 1 tablespoon salt
- 1 teaspoon black pepper
- vegetable oil

1. Using the largest holes on a box grater, grate the potatoes and place in a large bowl. When all of the potatoes have been grated, rinse with water. 2. Squeeze as much water out of the potatoes as possible and return to the bowl. 3. Add the onion powder, salt, and pepper to the bowl and stir to combine. 4. Preheat your griddle to medium heat and add a think layer of oil. Spread the potato mixture onto the grill creating a layer about ½ inch thick. Cook for approximately 8 minutes. 5. Working in sections using a large spatula, turn the potatoes and cook an additional 5 to 8 minutes or until both sides are golden brown. 6. Remove the potatoes from the griddle in sections and add to plates. Sprinkle with a pinch of salt and serve immediately.

Light and Fluffy Blueberry Pancakes

Prep time: 10 minutes | Cook time: 10 minutes | Serves 2

- 1 cup flour
- ¾ cup milk
- 2 tablespoons white vinegar
- 2 tablespoons sugar
- 1 teaspoon baking powder
- ½ teaspoon baking soda
- ½ teaspoon salt
- 1 egg
- 2 tablespoons butter, melted
- 1 cup fresh blueberries
- butter for cooking

1. In a bowl, combine the milk and vinegar. Set aside for two minutes. 2. In a large bowl, combine the flour, sugar, baking powder, baking soda, and salt. Stir in the milk, egg, blueberries, and melted butter. Mix until combined but not totally smooth. 3. Heat your griddle to medium heat and add a little butter. Pour the pancakes onto the griddle and cook until one side is golden brown. 4. Flip the pancakes and cook until the other side is golden. 5. Remove the pancakes from the griddle and serve with warm maple syrup.

Elegant Denver Omelet

Prep time: 5 minutes | Cook time: 10 minutes | Serves 2

- 6 large eggs
- ¼ cup country ham, diced
- ¼ cup yellow onion, finely chopped
- ¼ cup green bell pepper, chopped
- ⅔ cup cheddar cheese, shredded
- ¼ teaspoon cayenne pepper
- salt and black pepper
- 2 tablespoons butter

1. Heat your griddle to medium heat and place the butter onto the griddle. 2. Add the ham, onion, and pepper to the butter and cook until the vegetables have just softened. 3. Beat the eggs in a large bowl and add a pinch of salt and the cayenne pepper. 4. Split the vegetables into to portions on the griddle and add half of the eggs to each portion. Cook until the eggs have begun to firm up, and then add the cheese to each omelet. 5. Fold the omelets over and remove from the griddle. Serve immediately.

Chapter 1 Breakfasts

Chapter 2

Poultry

Chapter 2 Poultry

Chicken Fried Rice

Prep time: 10 minutes | Cook time: 20 minutes | Serves 4

- 2 boneless, skinless chicken breasts, cut into small pieces
- 1 cups long grain rice, cooked and allowed to air dry
- ⅓ cup soy sauce
- 1 yellow onion, finely chopped
- 1 cloves garlic, finely chopped
- 1 cups petite peas
- 1 carrots sliced into thin rounds
- ½ cup corn kernels
- ¼ cup vegetable oil
- 1 tablespoons butter

1. Heat the griddle to medium-high temperature. 2. Pour the vegetable oil onto the griddle surface. 3. Once the oil begins to shimmer, add the onion, carrot, peas, and corn. 4. Sauté the vegetables for a few minutes until they develop a light char. 5. Add the chicken pieces and cook until they are lightly browned. 6. Stir in the rice, soy sauce, garlic, and butter. 7. Toss everything together until the rice is tender and the vegetables are just soft enough. 8. Serve the dish right away while it's hot.

Chicken Breasts Griddle With Feta And Fresh Mint

Prep time: 5 minutes | Cook time: 14 minutes | Serves 4

- 2 whole skinless, boneless chicken breasts
- 1 piece (1½ ounces / 43 g) feta cheese, thinly sliced
- 8 fresh mint leaves, rinsed, blotted dry and cut into thin slivers
- Coarse salt (kosher or sea)
- Freshly ground black pepper
- tablespoon fresh lemon juice
- 1 tablespoon extra-virgin olive oil
- Lemon wedges, for serving

You'll also need:
- Wooden toothpicks

1. If you're using whole chicken breasts, slice each one in half. Trim off any sinew or excess fat, and discard the trimmings. Remove the tenders and set them aside. Place a half breast along the edge of a cutting board, and carefully cut a horizontal pocket into the breast, ensuring you don't cut through the edges. Repeat this for the remaining breast halves. Stuff each pocket with 2 or 3 slices of feta cheese and a few thin strips of mint leaves. Secure the pockets with lightly oiled toothpicks. 2. Arrange the chicken breasts in a baking dish just big enough to hold them comfortably. Season both sides with salt and pepper, then sprinkle any remaining mint over the top. Drizzle the lemon juice and olive oil over the chicken, gently patting it into the meat with your fingers to help the flavors soak in. 3. Cover the dish and let the chicken marinate in the refrigerator for 20 minutes, turning the pieces once or twice to ensure even marination. 4. Preheat the griddle by turning the control knob to the high setting. Once the griddle is hot, place the chicken breasts on it and cook for 10 to 14 minutes. To check for doneness, insert an instant-read thermometer into the thickest part of the chicken; the internal temperature should reach 160°F. 5. Transfer the cooked chicken breasts to a serving platter or individual plates, remove the toothpicks, and discard them. Serve the chicken immediately with lemon wedges on the side.

Buffalo Chicken Thighs

Prep time: 30 minutes | Cook time: hours | Serves 1

- 4-6 skinless, boneless chicken thighs
- Pork and poultry rub
- 4 tablespoons of butter
- 1 cup of sauce; buffalo wing
- Bleu cheese crumbles
- Ranch dressing

1. Preheat the griddle to 450°F with the lid closed to allow it to heat up fully. 2. Season the chicken thighs evenly with poultry rub, then place them on the griddle grate. 3. Cook the chicken for 8 to 10 minutes, flipping it once halfway through the cooking process. 4. Meanwhile, in a small saucepan over medium heat, combine the wing sauce and butter. Stir occasionally to prevent lumps from forming and to ensure a smooth sauce. 5. Once the chicken is cooked, dip each thigh into the wing sauce and butter mixture, making sure both sides are evenly coated. 6. Return the sauced chicken thighs to the griddle and cook for an additional 15 minutes, or until the internal temperature reaches 175°F. 7. Sprinkle bleu cheese over the chicken and drizzle with ranch dressing. 8. Serve immediately and enjoy!

Chicken Thighs With Ginger-Sesame Glaze

Prep time: 10 minutes | Cook time: 20 minutes | Serves 4-8

- 8 boneless, skinless chicken thighs

For the glaze:
- 3 tablespoons dark brown sugar
- 2½ tablespoons soy sauce
- 1 tablespoon fresh garlic, minced
- 1 teaspoon sesame seeds
- 1 teaspoon fresh ginger, minced
- 1 teaspoon sambal oelek
- ⅓ cup scallions, thinly sliced
- Non-stick cooking spray

1. In a large mixing bowl, combine all the glaze ingredients. Set aside half of the glaze for serving. 2. Add the chicken to the bowl and toss thoroughly to ensure it's well coated with the glaze. 3. Preheat the griddle to medium-high heat. 4. Lightly coat the griddle surface with cooking spray. 5. Place the chicken on the griddle and cook for about 6 minutes per side, or until fully cooked through. 6. Transfer the cooked chicken to serving plates and drizzle with the reserved glaze. Serve immediately and enjoy!

Honey Balsamic Marinated Chicken

Prep time: 30 minutes to 4 hours | Cook time: 20 minutes | Serves 4

- 2 pounds (907 g). boneless, skinless chicken thighs
- 1 teaspoon olive oil
- ½ teaspoon sea salt

For the Marinade:
- 2 tablespoons honey
- 2 tablespoons balsamic vinegar
- ¼ teaspoon black pepper
- ½ teaspoon paprika
- ¾ teaspoon onion powder
- 2 tablespoons tomato paste
- 1 teaspoon garlic, minced

1. Place the chicken, olive oil, salt, black pepper, paprika, and onion powder in a sealable plastic bag. Seal the bag and shake well to evenly coat the chicken with the seasoning and oil; set aside. 2. In a bowl, whisk together the balsamic vinegar, tomato paste, garlic, and honey until well combined. 3. Split the marinade into two portions. Pour one portion into the bag with the chicken, and store the other half in a sealed container in the refrigerator. 4. Reseal the bag and shake again to coat the chicken thoroughly. Let it marinate in the refrigerator for at least 30 minutes or up to 4 hours. 5. Preheat the griddle to medium-high heat. 6. Discard the bag and used marinade. Place the chicken on the griddle and cook for 7 minutes per side, or until the juices run clear and the internal temperature reaches 165°F (74°C). 7. In the final minute of cooking, brush the reserved marinade over the chicken thighs. 8. Remove from the griddle and serve immediately. Enjoy!

Sizzling Chicken Fajitas

Prep time: 5 minutes | Cook time: 25 minutes | Serves 4

- 4 boneless chicken breast halves, thinly sliced
- 1 yellow onion, sliced
- 1 large green bell pepper, sliced
- 1 large red bell pepper, sliced
- 1 teaspoon ground cumin
- 1 teaspoon garlic powder
- 1 teaspoon onion powder
- 2 tablespoons lime juice
- 1 tablespoon olive oil
- ½ teaspoon black pepper
- 1 teaspoon salt
- 3 tablespoons vegetable oil
- 10 flour tortillas

1. Place the chicken, cumin, garlic, onion, lime juice, salt, pepper, and olive oil in a zipperlock bag. Seal the bag and shake to coat the chicken thoroughly. Let it marinate for 30 minutes. 2. Preheat the griddle to medium heat. 3. Drizzle olive oil on one side of the griddle and heat until it starts to shimmer. Add the sliced onion and pepper, cooking until they are slightly softened. 4. On the other side of the griddle, place the marinated chicken and cook until it begins to brown lightly. 5. Once the chicken is browned, mix it with the onions and peppers, and continue cooking until the chicken reaches an internal temperature of 165°F (74°C). 6. Remove the chicken and vegetables from the griddle and serve immediately with warm tortillas. Enjoy!

Chicken Roast with Pineapple Salsa

Prep time: 10 minutes | Cook time: 45 minutes | Serves 2

- ¼ cup extra virgin olive oil
- ¼ cup freshly chopped cilantro
- avocado, diced
- 1 pound (454 g) boneless chicken breasts
- 1 cups canned pineapples
- 2 teaspoons honey
- Juice from 1 lime
- Salt and pepper to taste

1. Season the chicken breasts with lime juice, olive oil, honey, salt, and pepper. Preheat the griddle to high heat. Once the griddle is hot, place the chicken on the surface and cook for 45 minutes, flipping every 10 minutes to ensure all sides are evenly cooked. 2. When the chicken is done, serve it with fresh pineapple slices, chopped cilantro, and avocado. Enjoy!

Chapter 2 Poultry

Chicken and Vegetable Kebabs

Prep time: 5 minutes | Cook time: 15 minutes | Serves 4

- 1½ to 2 pounds (0.68 kg-0.9 kg) boneless, skinless chicken breasts or thighs
- 2 cups cherry or grape tomatoes
- 3 tablespoons good-quality olive oil
- Salt and pepper

1. If using bamboo or wooden skewers, soak them in water for 30 minutes to prevent burning. Cut the chicken into pieces that are about 1 to 1½ inches, depending on the size of the tomatoes. In a medium bowl, toss the chicken and tomatoes with oil, then season with salt and pepper. Thread the chicken and tomatoes onto the skewers, alternating between the two. 2. Place the skewers on the hot griddle and cook for 10 to 15 minutes, turning occasionally, until the chicken is cooked through and no longer pink in the center. Transfer the skewers to a serving platter and serve hot or at room temperature. Enjoy!

Chicken Satay With Thai Peanut Sauce

Prep time: 5 minutes | Cook time: 8 minutes | Serves 4

- 3 large boneless skinless chicken breasts or 6 boneless skinless thighs
- satay sticks

Thai Peanut Sauce:
- cup creamy peanut butter
- ¾ cup coconut milk
- 1 tablespoon soy sauce
- 1 tablespoon fresh lime juice
- 1 tablespoon brown sugar
- 2 tablespoon sesame oil
- 2 teaspoons.crushed red pepper flakes
- 1 tablespoon fish sauce
- 1 tablespoon sriracha sauce
- 1 (3-in.) piece of ginger, peeled and diced
- 2 cloves garlic, minced
- ¼ cup chopped cilantro

1. Cut the chicken into 1.5-inch squares and thread them onto satay sticks. Lightly season the chicken with salt. In a saucepan, combine all the sauce ingredients except the cilantro. Place the saucepan over medium heat, whisking the ingredients together, and let it simmer for 5 minutes. Once the flavors are well blended, use a blender or immersion blender to puree the sauce until smooth. Pour the sauce into a bowl and garnish with cilantro. 2. Preheat the griddle to high heat by turning the control knob to the high setting. Once the griddle is hot, place the chicken skewers on the surface and cook for 8 minutes, turning as needed. Since the chicken pieces are small, they will cook quickly, but ensure the internal temperature reaches at least 165°F to avoid undercooked chicken. Remove the skewers from the griddle and serve with the prepared sauce and a sprinkle of fresh cilantro. Enjoy!

Hoisin Turkey Wings

Prep time: 15 minutes | Cook time: 1 hour | Serves 8

- 2 pounds (0.9 kg) turkey wings
- ½ cup hoisin sauce
- 1 tablespoon honey
- 2 teaspoons soy sauce
- 2 garlic cloves (minced)
- 1 teaspoon freshly grated ginger
- 2 teaspoons sesame oil
- 1 teaspoon pepper or to taste
- 1 teaspoon salt or to taste
- ¼ cup pineapple juice
- 1 tablespoon chopped green onions
- 1 tablespoon sesame seeds
- 1 lemon (cut into wedges)

1. In a large container, mix together honey, garlic, ginger, soy sauce, hoisin sauce, sesame oil, salt, and pepper. Pour the mixture into a ziplock bag, add the wings, seal the bag, and toss to coat thoroughly. Refrigerate for 2 hours to allow the flavors to develop. 2. Take the wings out of the marinade and set the marinade aside. Let the wings rest until they reach room temperature. Preheat the griddle to 300°F, keeping the lid closed for 15 minutes. 3. Place the wings in a grilling basket and set the basket on the griddle. 4. Cook the wings for 1 hour, or until their internal temperature reaches 165°F. 5. While the wings are cooking, pour the reserved marinade into a saucepan over medium-high heat. Add the pineapple juice and stir well. Bring the mixture to a boil, then lower the heat and simmer until the sauce thickens. Brush the thickened sauce onto the wings and cook for an additional 6 minutes. 6. Remove the wings from the griddle, garnish with green onions, sesame seeds, and lemon wedges, then serve immediately. Enjoy!

Rosemary Butter Cornish Hens

Prep time: 10 minutes | Cook time: 1 hour | Serves 2

- 1 cornish hen, rinse and pat dry with paper towels
- 1 tablespoon butter, melted
- 1 rosemary sprigs
- 1 teaspoon poultry seasoning

1. Stuff rosemary sprigs into the hen cavity. 2. Brush hen with melted butter and season with poultry seasoning. 3. Preheat the griddle to high heat. 4. Spray griddle top with cooking spray. 5. Place hen on hot griddle top and cook for 60 minutes or until the internal temperature of hens reaches 165°F. 6. Slice and serve.

Chapter 2 Poultry 15

Caesar Marinated Griddle Chicken

Prep time: 10 minutes | Cook time: 24 minutes | Serves 3

- ¼ cup crouton
- 1 teaspoon lemon zest. Form into ovals, skewer and griddle.
- ½ cup Parmesan
- ¼ cup breadcrumbs
- 1 pound (454 g) ground chicken
- 1 tablespoons Caesar dressing and more for drizzling
- 2-4 romaine leaves

1. In a shallow dish, combine the chicken, 2 tablespoons of Caesar dressing, parmesan, and breadcrumbs. Use your hands to mix everything thoroughly until well combined. Shape the mixture into 1-inch oval patties. 2. Thread the chicken patties onto skewers. Preheat the griddle to high heat. Once the griddle is hot, place the skewers on the surface and cook for 12 minutes, turning the skewers halfway through the cooking time. Serve the skewers on a bed of lettuce, garnish with croutons, and drizzle with extra Caesar dressing. Enjoy!

Cured Turkey Drumstick

Prep time: 20 minutes | Cook time: 2.5 to 3 hours | Serves 3

- 3 fresh or thawed frozen turkey drumsticks
- 3 tablespoons extra virgin olive oil
- Brine component
- 4 cups of filtered water
- ¼ cup kosher salt
- ¼ cup brown sugar
- 1 teaspoon garlic powder
- poultry seasoning 1 teaspoon
- ½ teaspoon red pepper flakes
- 1 teaspoon pink hardened salt

1. Combine the salt water ingredients in a 1-gallon sealable bag. Submerge the turkey drumstick in the salt water, seal the bag, and refrigerate for 12 hours. Afterward, take the drumstick out of the brine, rinse it thoroughly with cold water, and pat it dry using a paper towel. 2. Allow the drumstick to air dry in the refrigerator, uncovered, for 2 hours. Take it out and rub a tablespoon of extra virgin olive oil both under the skin and over the surface of each drumstick. 3. Prepare the griddle for indirect cooking and preheat it to 250°F. 4. Place the drumstick on the griddle and smoke at 250°F for 2 hours. After 2 hours, increase the griddle temperature to 325°F. 5. Continue cooking the drumstick at 325°F until the internal temperature of the thickest part reaches 180°F, as measured with an instant-read digital thermometer. 6. Once done, tent the smoked turkey drumstick loosely with foil and let it rest for 15 minutes before serving. Enjoy!

Slow Roasted Shawarma

Prep time: 30 minutes | Cook time: 4 hours | Serves 1

- 5½ pounds (2.5 kg) of chicken thighs; boneless, skinless
- 4½ pounds (2.04 kg) of lamb fat
- Pita bread
- 5½ pounds (2.5 kg) of top sirloin
- 2 yellow onions; large
- 4 tablespoons of rub
- Desired toppings like pickles, tomatoes, fries, salad and more

1. Slice the meat and fat into ½-inch thick pieces and divide them into 3 separate bowls. 2. Season each bowl with the rub, massaging the seasoning thoroughly into the meat to ensure it penetrates well. 3. Place half an onion at the base of each half skewer to create a stable foundation. 4. Layer the meat by adding 2 layers from each bowl at a time, stacking them carefully. 5. Try to build the stack as evenly and symmetrically as possible. 6. Finish by placing the remaining half onions on top of the stack. 7. Wrap the entire skewer tightly in plastic wrap and refrigerate it overnight to let the flavors meld. 8. Preheat the griddle to 275°F. 9. Position the shawarma on the griddle grate and cook for approximately 4 hours, turning it at least once during the process. 10. Once cooked, remove the shawarma from the griddle and increase the temperature to 445°F. 11. Place a cast iron griddle on the griddle grate and drizzle it with olive oil. 12. When the cast iron is hot, place the entire shawarma on it and smoke for 5 to 10 minutes on each side until nicely charred. 13. Remove the shawarma from the griddle and slice off the crispy edges. 14. Repeat the same process with the remaining shawarma. 15. Serve the sliced shawarma in pita bread with your favorite toppings. Enjoy!

Flavorful Cornish Game Hen

Prep time: 10 minutes | Cook time: 60 minutes | Serves 2

- 1 cornish game hen
- ½ tablespoon olive oil
- ¼ tablespoon poultry seasoning

1. Coat the hen with oil and evenly rub it with poultry seasoning. 2. Preheat the griddle to high heat. 3. Lightly spray the griddle surface with cooking spray. 4. Place the hen on the hot griddle and cook on all sides until nicely browned. 5. Cover the hen with a lid or an inverted pan, and cook for 60 minutes or until the internal temperature reaches 180°F. 6. Once done, slice the hen and serve immediately. Enjoy!

Chipotle Adobe Chicken

Prep time: 1-24 hours | Cook time: 20 minutes | Serves 4-6

- 2 pounds (0.9 kg) chicken thighs or breasts (boneless, skinless)

For the marinade:
- ¼ cup olive oil
- 2 chipotle peppers, in adobo sauce, plus 1 teaspoon adobo sauce from the can
- 1 tablespoon garlic, minced
- 1 shallot, finely chopped
- 1½ tablespoons cumin
- 1 tablespoon cilantro, superfinely chopped or dried
- 1 teaspoon chili powder
- 1 teaspoon dried oregano
- ½ teaspoon salt
- Fresh limes, garnish
- Cilantro, garnish

1. Preheat the griddle to medium-high heat. 2. In a food processor or blender, combine all the marinade ingredients and blend until a smooth paste forms. 3. Transfer the chicken and marinade to a sealable plastic bag, seal it tightly, and massage the bag to evenly coat the chicken. 4. Place the bag in the refrigerator and let the chicken marinate for at least 1 hour, or up to 24 hours for more intense flavor. 5. Once ready to cook, sear the chicken on the hot griddle for 7 minutes, then flip and cook for another 7 minutes. 6. Lower the heat and continue cooking until the internal temperature of the chicken reaches 165°F. Remove the chicken from the griddle and let it rest for 5 to 10 minutes. 7. Finish with a squeeze of fresh lime juice and a sprinkle of chopped cilantro before serving. Enjoy!

Hasselback Stuffed Chicken

Prep time: 15 minutes | Cook time: 30 minutes | Serves 4

- 4 boneless, skinless chicken breasts
- 2 tablespoons olive oil
- 2 tablespoons taco seasoning
- ½ red, yellow and green pepper, very thinly sliced
- 1 small red onion, very thinly sliced
- ½ cup Mexican shredded cheese
- Guacamole, for serving
- Sour cream, for serving
- Salsa, for serving

1. Preheat the griddle to medium-high heat. 2. Make thin, horizontal slits across each chicken breast, similar to how you would slice hasselback potatoes. 3. Rub the chicken breasts evenly with olive oil and taco seasoning, ensuring the seasoning gets into the slits. 4. Stuff each cut with a combination of bell pepper slices and red onion. Place the chicken breasts on the hot griddle. 5. Cook the chicken for 15 minutes, allowing it to cook through and develop a golden sear. 6. Take the chicken off the heat briefly and sprinkle cheese over the top. 7. Tent the chicken loosely with foil and cook for an additional 5 minutes, or until the cheese is fully melted. 8. Remove the chicken from the griddle and garnish with guacamole, sour cream, and salsa. Serve with your favorite sides and enjoy!

Smoked Chicken in Maple Flavor

Prep time: 30 minutes | Cook time: 6 hours | Serves 1

- 5 pounds (2.3 kg) boneless chicken breast (s)
- the spice
- 1 tablespoon chipotle powder
- 1½ teaspoons salt
- 2 teaspoons garlic powder
- 2 teaspoons onion powder
- 1 teaspoon pepper
- the glaze
- ½ cup maple syrup

1. Heat the griddle to 225°F. 2. In a bowl, combine the chipotle, salt, garlic powder, onion powder, and pepper, mixing until evenly blended. 3. Coat the chicken thoroughly with the spice mixture, then place it on the griddle's rack. 4. Smoke the chicken for 4 hours, brushing it with maple syrup every hour to enhance the flavor. 5. Once the internal temperature reaches 160°F (71°C), take the smoked chicken breast off the griddle and transfer it to a serving dish. 6. Serve immediately and enjoy the smoky goodness!

Orange Cornish Hen

Prep time: 10 minutes | Cook time: 1 hour | Serves 2

- 1 cornish hen
- ¼ onion, cut into chunks
- ¼ orange cut into wedges

For glaze:
- 2-star anise
- 1 tablespoon honey
- 1 cup orange juice
- ¼ fresh orange, sliced
- 2 garlic cloves
- 4 fresh sage leaves
- 1½ fresh rosemary sprigs
- ½ orange zest
- 1½ ounces (43 g) Grand Marnier
- ½ cinnamon stick

1. Fill the cavity of the hen with orange wedges, garlic cloves, onion pieces, and your choice of herbs. Season generously with salt and pepper. 2. Heat the griddle to a high temperature. 3. Lightly spray the griddle surface with cooking oil to prevent sticking. 4. Place the hen on the hot griddle and cook for about 60 minutes, or until the internal temperature reaches 165°F. 5. While the hen is cooking, prepare the glaze by simmering all the glaze ingredients in a saucepan over medium-high heat until the mixture thickens and reduces by half. 6. Brush the hen thoroughly with the glaze to coat it evenly. 7. Carve the hen into slices and serve immediately.

Sage Thyme Cornish Hen

Prep time: 10 minutes | Cook time: 1 hour | Serves 2

- 1 cornish hen
- ½ tablespoon paprika
- ¼ teaspoon pepper
- ¼ teaspoon sage
- ½ teaspoon thyme
- ½ tablespoon onion powder

1. Combine paprika, onion powder, thyme, sage, and pepper in a small bowl and mix well. 2. Evenly rub the seasoning mixture all over the hen, ensuring it is thoroughly coated. 3. Preheat the griddle to high heat. 4. Lightly spray the surface of the griddle with cooking spray to prevent sticking. 5. Place the hen on the hot griddle and cook for about 60 minutes, or until the internal temperature reaches 185°F. 6. Once cooked, serve the hen immediately and enjoy.

Tarragon Chicken Tenders

Prep time: 5 minutes | Cook time: 5 minutes | Serves 4

for the chicken:
- 1½ pounds (680 g) chicken tenders (12 to 16 tenders)
- coarse salt (kosher or sea) and freshly ground black pepper
- 3 tablespoons chopped fresh tarragon

for the sauce (optional):
- 2 tablespoons fresh lemon juice
- 2 tablespoons salted butter
- leaves, plus 4 whole sprigs for garnish
- teaspoon finely grated lemon zest
- 1 tablespoons fresh lemon juice
- 2 tablespoons extra-virgin olive oil
- ½ cup heavy (whipping) cream

1. To prepare the chicken, arrange the chicken tenders in a nonreactive baking dish, making sure they fit in a single layer. 2. Generously season both sides of the tenders with salt and pepper. Evenly sprinkle the chopped tarragon and lemon zest over the tenders, gently pressing them in with your fingertips. Drizzle the lemon juice and olive oil over the tenders, patting the mixture onto the chicken to coat well. Cover and let the chicken marinate in the refrigerator for 10 minutes. When ready, lift each tender with tongs, allowing excess marinade to drip off, and discard the remaining marinade. 3. Preheat the griddle to high heat. Once the surface is hot, lay the chicken tenders on the griddle and cook for 3 to 5 minutes. To check if they're done, press lightly on the tenders; they should feel firm when fully cooked. 4. Move the cooked chicken tenders to a serving platter or individual plates. If you are making the sauce, combine the lemon juice and butter in a small saucepan or directly on the griddle pan over medium heat. Stir in the cream and bring the mixture to a boil, scraping up any browned bits from the pan with a wooden spoon. Let the sauce boil and thicken for about 3 to 5 minutes. Pour the lemon cream sauce over the chicken tenders and serve immediately.

BBQ Hen

Prep time: 10 minutes | Cook time: 1 hour 30 minutes | Serves 8

- 1 cornish hen
- 2 tablespoons BBQ rub

1. Heat the griddle to high heat. 2. Lightly spray the griddle surface with cooking spray to prevent sticking. 3. Evenly coat the hens with BBQ rub, then place them on the hot griddle. Cook for about 1½ hours, or until the internal temperature reaches 165°F. 4. Once cooked, slice the hens and serve immediately. Enjoy!

Bone-In Chicken Thighs with Caramelized Fish Sauce

Prep time: 10 minutes | Cook time: 55 minutes | Serves 4

- 3 pounds (1.36 kg) bone-in, skin-on chicken thighs
- Salt and pepper
- ¼ cup fish sauce
- 2 tablespoons turbinado sugar
- 1 tablespoon minced garlic
- dried red chiles

1. Trim any excess fat and skin from the chicken thighs, making sure not to expose the meat. Season both sides with salt and pepper. 2. Turn the control knob to high and allow the griddle to heat up. Once hot, place the chicken thighs on the griddle, skin side up, and cook for about 20 minutes. Flip the thighs and rotate them 180 degrees to ensure even browning. Continue cooking until the meat is no longer pink at the bone, about 40 to 55 minutes total, depending on the size of the pieces. 3. While the chicken is cooking, combine the fish sauce, sugar, garlic, and chiles in a small saucepan over low heat. Stir until the sugar completely dissolves. Let the sauce cool slightly, then pour it into a large heatproof bowl and remove the chiles. 4. Once the thighs are fully cooked, transfer them to the bowl and toss with the glaze, using tongs to coat evenly. Set the griddle to medium heat. 5. Take the thighs out of the glaze, allowing any excess to drip off, and place them skin side up on the griddle. Cook for 1 to 3 minutes per side, turning once, until the skin is crispy and browned. If the glaze starts to burn, move the thighs away from direct heat. 6. Transfer the thighs to a serving platter and enjoy!

Classic BBQ Chicken

Prep time: 5 minutes | Cook time: 1 hour 45 minutes | Serves 4-6

- 4 pounds (1.8 kg) of your favorite chicken, including legs, thighs, wings, and breasts, skin-on
- Salt
- Olive oil
- 1 cup barbecue sauce, like Hickory Mesquite or homemade

1. Rub the chicken with olive oil and salt. 2. Preheat the griddle to high heat. 3. Sear chicken skin side down on the grill for 5-10 minutes. 4. Turn the griddle down to medium low heat, tent with foil and cook for 30 minutes. 5. Turn chicken and baste with barbecue sauce. 6. Cover the chicken again and allow to cook for another 20 minutes. 7. Baste, cover and cook again for 30 minutes; repeat basting and turning during this time. 8. The chicken is done when the internal temperature of the chicken pieces are 165°F (74°C) and juices run clear. 9. Baste with more barbecue sauce to serve!

Jalapeno Injection Turkey

Prep time: 15 minutes | Cook time: 4 hours 10 minutes | Serves 4

- 15 pounds (6.8 kg) whole turkey, giblet removed
- ½ of medium red onion, peeled and minced
- 8 jalapeño peppers
- 2 tablespoons minced garlic
- 4 tablespoons garlic powder
- 6 tablespoons Italian seasoning
- 1 cup butter, softened, unsalted
- ¼ cup olive oil
- 1 cup chicken broth

1. Open the griddle hopper and fill it with dry pellets. Ensure the ash-can is properly in place. Open the ash damper, power on the griddle, and then close the ash damper. 2. Set the griddle temperature to 200°F and allow it to preheat for 30 minutes, or until the green light on the dial blinks, indicating the set temperature has been reached. 3. While the griddle is preheating, place a large saucepan over medium-high heat. Add the oil and butter. Once the butter has melted, add the onion, garlic, and peppers, and cook for 3 to 5 minutes until they turn a nice golden brown. 4. Pour in the broth, stir thoroughly, and let the mixture boil for 5 minutes. Take the saucepan off the heat and strain the mixture, keeping only the liquid. 5. Using the prepared liquid, inject the turkey generously. Spray the outside of the turkey with butter spray and season it thoroughly with garlic and Italian seasoning. 6. Place the turkey on the griddle, close the lid, and smoke for 30 minutes. Then, raise the temperature to 325°F and continue smoking the turkey for about 3 hours, or until the internal temperature reaches 165°F. 7. Once cooked, move the turkey to a cutting board and let it rest for 5 minutes. Carve the turkey into slices and serve immediately.

Sweet Chili Lime Chicken

Prep time: 35 minutes | Cook time: 15 minutes | Serves 4

- ½ cup sweet chili sauce
- ¼ cup soy sauce
- 1 teaspoon mirin
- 1 teaspoon orange juice, fresh squeezed
- 1 teaspoon orange marmalade
- 2 tablespoons lime juice
- 1 tablespoon brown sugar
- 1 clove garlic, minced
- 4 boneless, skinless chicken breasts
- Sesame seeds, for garnish

1. In a small mixing bowl, whisk together the sweet chili sauce, soy sauce, mirin, orange marmalade, lime juice, orange juice, brown sugar, and minced garlic until well combined. 2. Reserve ¼ cup of the sauce and set it aside for later use. 3. Toss the chicken in the remaining sauce, making sure it's well coated, and let it marinate for 30 minutes. 4. Preheat the griddle to medium heat. 5. Place the chicken on the griddle and cook for 7 minutes per side, or until fully cooked. 6. Brush the cooked chicken with the reserved marinade, sprinkle with sesame seeds, and serve with your favorite sides. Enjoy!

Savory Chicken Burgers

Prep time: 10 minutes | Cook time: 20 minutes | Serves 3

- 1 pound (454 g) ground chicken
- ½ red onion, finely chopped
- 1 teaspoon garlic powder
- ½ teaspoon onion powder
- ¼ teaspoon black pepper
- ½ teaspoon salt
- 3 tablespoons vegetable oil
- 3 potato buns, toasted

1. In a large bowl, mix together the ground chicken, chopped onion, garlic powder, onion powder, pepper, and salt until well combined. Gently shape the mixture into three equal patties, being careful not to overwork the meat to keep the burgers light and tender. 2. Preheat the griddle to medium-high heat and add the vegetable oil. 3. Once the oil is shimmering, place the chicken patties on the griddle and cook for 5 minutes on each side, or until the internal temperature reaches 165°F. 4. Take the patties off the griddle and let them rest for 5 minutes. Serve the patties on toasted buns with your favorite toppings. Enjoy!

Turkey Pesto Panini

Prep time: 5 minutes | Cook time: 6 minutes | Serves 2

- 1 tablespoon olive oil
- slices French bread
- ½ cup pesto sauce
- slices mozzarella cheese
- 2 cups chopped leftover turkey
- 1 Roma tomato, thinly sliced
- 1 avocado, halved, seeded, peeled and sliced

1. Preheat the griddle to medium-high heat. 2. Brush one side of each bread slice with olive oil. 3. Place 2 slices of bread, olive oil side down, onto the hot griddle. 4. Spread 2 tablespoons of pesto over the exposed side of each slice of bread. 5. Layer the sandwich by adding a slice of mozzarella, turkey, tomato slices, avocado, and another slice of mozzarella. Complete the sandwich by placing another slice of bread on top, olive oil side facing up. Repeat this process with the remaining ingredients. 6. Cook the sandwiches until the bread turns golden brown and the cheese melts, about 2-3 minutes per side. 7. Serve the sandwiches warm alongside your favorite salad or soup. Enjoy!

Hot Sauce Smoked Turkey Tabasco

Prep time: 20 minutes | Cook time: 4 hours 15 minutes | Serves 8

- 4 pounds (1.8 kg)whole turkey
- For the rub
- ¼ cup brown sugar
- 2 teaspoons smoked paprika
- 1 teaspoon salt
- 1½ teaspoons onion powder
- 2 teaspoons oregano
- 2 teaspoons garlic powder
- ½ teaspoon dried thyme
- ½ teaspoon white pepper
- ½ teaspoon cayenne pepper
- The Glaze
- ½ cup ketchup
- ½ cup hot sauce
- 1 tablespoon cider vinegar
- 2 teaspoons tabasco
- ½ teaspoon cajun spices
- 3 tablespoons unsalted butter

1. Coat the turkey with 2 tablespoons of brown sugar, smoked paprika, salt, onion powder, garlic powder, dried thyme, white pepper, and cayenne pepper. Let the turkey rest for 1 hour to allow the flavors to penetrate. 2. Prepare the griddle for indirect heat and preheat it to 275°F (135°C). 3. Place the seasoned turkey on the griddle and smoke it for 4 hours. 4. While the turkey is smoking, combine ketchup, hot sauce, cider vinegar, Tabasco, and Cajun spices in a saucepan. Bring the mixture to a gentle simmer over medium heat. 5. Remove the saucepan from the heat and immediately stir in the unsalted butter until it melts completely. 6. After 4 hours, brush the turkey with the prepared Tabasco sauce and smoke for an additional 15 minutes. 7. When the internal temperature of the turkey reaches 170°F (77°C), take it off the griddle and transfer it to a serving dish. Enjoy!

Chicken Fajitas

Prep time: 10 minutes | Cook time: 15 minutes | Serves 4

- boneless, skinless chicken breasts, sliced
- small red onion, sliced
- red bell peppers, sliced
- ½ cup spicy ranch salad dressing, divided
- ½ teaspoon dried oregano
- 8 corn tortillas
- 1 cups torn butter lettuce
- avocados, peeled and chopped

1. In a bowl, combine the chicken, onion, and pepper. Drizzle with 1 tablespoon of salad dressing, sprinkle with oregano, and toss until everything is evenly coated. 2. Preheat the griddle to high heat. Once it's hot, place the chicken and vegetables on the griddle and cook for 10 to 14 minutes, or until the chicken reaches an internal temperature of 165°F on a food thermometer. 3. Transfer the cooked chicken and vegetables to a bowl and toss with the remaining salad dressing. 4. Serve the chicken mixture alongside tortillas, lettuce, and avocado slices, allowing everyone to assemble their own wraps. Enjoy!

Smoked Whole Turkey

Prep time: 10 minutes | Cook time: 5 hours | Serves 6

- 1 (10-12 pounds / 4.5 kg-5.4 kg) turkey, giblets removed
- Extra-virgin olive oil, for rubbing
- ¼ cup poultry seasoning
- 8 tablespoons (1 stick) unsalted butter, melted
- ½ cup apple juice
- 2 teaspoons dried sage
- 2 teaspoons dried thyme

1. Follow the manufacturer's instructions to start your griddle. Preheat it with the lid closed to 250°F. 2. Rub the turkey thoroughly with oil and season it generously with poultry seasoning, making sure to get some seasoning under the skin as well. 3. In a bowl, mix together the melted butter, apple juice, sage, and thyme to create a basting mixture. 4. Place the turkey in a roasting pan and set it on the griddle. Close the lid and cook for 5 to 6 hours, basting the turkey every hour. Continue cooking until the skin is brown and crispy, and a meat thermometer inserted into the thickest part of the thigh reads 165°F. 5. Allow the turkey to rest for 15 to 20 minutes before carving. Enjoy your meal!

Turkey Legs

Prep time: 10 minutes | Cook time: 5 hours | Serves 4

- 4 turkey legs- For the Brine:
- ½ cup curing salt
- 1 tablespoon whole black peppercorns- 1 cup BBQ rub
- ½ cup brown sugar
- 2 bay leaves
- 2 teaspoons liquid smoke
- 16 cups of warm water
- 4 cups ice-8 cups of cold water

1. To prepare the brine, take a large stockpot and place it over high heat. Pour in warm water, then add peppercorns, bay leaves, and liquid smoke. 2. Stir in the salt, sugar, and BBQ rub, and bring the mixture to a boil. 3. Remove the pot from the heat and let it cool to room temperature. Add cold water and ice cubes to the pot, then place the brine in the refrigerator to chill. Once chilled, fully submerge the turkey legs in the brine and let them soak for 24 hours in the refrigerator. 4. After 24 hours, take the turkey legs out of the brine, rinse them thoroughly, and pat dry with paper towels. 5. When you're ready to cook, turn on the griddle and set the temperature to 250°F. Let it preheat for at least 15 minutes. 6. Once the griddle is preheated, open the lid, place the turkey legs on the griddle grate, and close the lid. Smoke the turkey legs for 5 hours, or until they are nicely browned and the internal temperature reaches 165°F. Serve immediately and enjoy!

BBQ Pulled Turkey Sandwiches

Prep time: 30 minutes | Cook time: 4 hours | Serves 1

- 6 skin-on turkey thighs
- 6 split and buttered buns
- 1½ cups of chicken broth
- 1 cup of BBQ sauce
- Poultry rub

1. Season both sides of the turkey thighs generously with poultry rub. 2. Preheat the griddle to 180°F. 3. Place the turkey thighs on the griddle grate and smoke for 30 minutes. 4. After 30 minutes, transfer the thighs to a disposable aluminum foil tray and pour the brine around the thighs. 5. Cover the tray with a lid or tightly with foil. 6. Increase the griddle temperature to 325°F and continue roasting the turkey thighs until the internal temperature reaches 180°F. 7. Once done, remove the foil tray from the griddle, but keep the griddle on. 8. Allow the turkey thighs to cool slightly. 9. Pour the drippings into a separate container and set aside. 10. Remove and discard the skin from the turkey thighs. 11. Shred the meat using forks and place it back into the foil tray. 12. Add 1 cup of BBQ sauce and a bit more of the reserved drippings to the shredded meat. 13. Cover the tray with a lid or foil, and reheat the turkey on the griddle for another 30 minutes. Serve warm and enjoy!

Kale Caesar Salad With Seared Chicken

Prep time: 10 minutes | Cook time: 8 minutes | Serves 1

- 1 chicken breast
- 1 teaspoon garlic powder
- ½ teaspoon black pepper

For the dressing:

- 1 tablespoon mayonnaise
- ½ tablespoon dijon mustard
- ½ teaspoon garlic powder
- ½ teaspoon worcestershire sauce
- ½ teaspoon sea salt
- 2 kale leaves, chopped
- shaved parmesan, for serving
- ¼ lemon, juice of (or ½ a small lime)
- ¼ teaspoon anchovy paste
- Pinch of sea salt
- Pinch of black pepper

1. In a small mixing bowl, combine garlic powder, black pepper, and sea salt. Evenly coat the chicken breasts with the seasoning mixture. 2. Preheat the griddle to medium-high heat. 3. Once the griddle is hot, sear the chicken for 7 minutes on each side, or until a meat thermometer inserted into the thickest part of the breast reads 165°F (74°C). 4. While the chicken cooks, whisk together all the dressing ingredients in a separate bowl until smooth. 5. Arrange the kale on a serving plate, drizzle the dressing over it, and toss until the leaves are evenly coated. 6. Slice the chicken breasts diagonally and lay the pieces on top of the salad. Garnish with shaved parmesan and serve immediately.

Chapter 3
Fish and Seafood

Chapter 3 Fish and Seafood

Grilled Cuttlefish and Spinach Pine Nut Medley

Prep time: 15 minutes | Cook time: 30 minutes | Serves 6

- ½ cup of olive oil
- 1 tablespoon of lemon juice
- 1 teaspoon oregano
- Pinch of salt
- 8 large cuttlefish, cleaned
- Spinach, pine nuts, olive oil and vinegar for serving
- Intolerances:
- Gluten-Free
- Egg-Free
- Lactose-Free

1. Prepare marinade with olive oil, lemon juice, oregano and a pinch of salt pepper (be careful, cuttlefish do not need too much salt). 2. Place the cuttlefish in the marinade, tossing to cover evenly. Cover and marinate for about 1 hour. 3. Remove the cuttlefish from marinade and pat dry them on paper towel. 4. Start the griddle, and set the temperature to high and preheat, lid closed, for 10 to 15 minutes. 5. Griddle the cuttlefish just 3 - 4 minutes on each side. 6. Serve hot with spinach, pine nuts, olive oil, and vinegar.

Seared Sea Scallops with Corn Medley

Prep time: 25 minutes | Cook time: 30 minutes | Serves 6

- 6 shucked ears of corn
- 1-pint grape tomatoes, halved
- 3 sliced scallions, white and light green parts only
- ⅓ cup basil leaves, finely shredded
- Salt and grounded pepper
- 1 small shallot, minced

Intolerances:
- Gluten-Free
- Egg-Free
- 2 tablespoons balsamic vinegar
- 2 tablespoons hot water
- 1 teaspoon Dijon mustard ¼ cup
- 3 tablespoon sunflower oil
- 1½ pounds (680 g) sea scallops

- Lactose-Free

1. In a pot of boiling salted water, cook the corn for about 5 minutes. Drain and cool. 2. Place the corn into a big bowl and cut off the kernels. Add the tomatoes, the scallions and basil then season with salt and grounded pepper. 3. In a blender, mix the minced shallot with the vinegar, heated water, and mustard. With the blender on, gradually add 6 tablespoon of the sunflower oil. 4. Season the vinaigrette with salt and pepper; at that point, add it to the corn salad. 5. In a huge bowl, toss the remaining 1 tablespoon of oil with the scallops, then season with salt and grounded pepper. 6. Heat a griddle pan. Put on half of the scallops and griddle over high heat, turning once, until singed, around 4 minutes. 7. Repeat with the other half of the scallops. Place the corn salad on plates, then top with the scallops and serve.

Seared Calamari with Herb Mustard Sauce

Prep time: 10 minutes | Cook time: 35 minutes | Serves 6

- 8 Calamari, cleaned
- 2 cups of milk
- Sauce
- 4 teaspoon of sweet mustard
- Juice from 2 lemons
- ½ cup of olive oil
- 2 tablespoons fresh oregano, finely chopped
- Pepper, ground
- ½ bunch of parsley, finely chopped

Intolerances:
- Gluten-Free
- Egg-Free
- Lactose-Free

1. Clean calamari well and cut into slices. 2. Place calamari in a large metal bow, cover and marinate with milk overnight. 3. Remove calamari from the milk and drain well on paper towel. Grease the fish lightly with olive oil. 4. In a bowl, combine mustard and the juice from the two lemons. 5. Beat lightly and pour the olive oil very slowly; stir until all the ingredients are combined well. 6. Add the oregano and pepper and stir well. 7. Start the griddle and set the temperature to moderate; preheat, lid closed, for 10 to 15 minutes. 8. Place the calamari on the griddle and cook for 2-3 minutes per side or until it has a bit of char and remove from the griddle. 9. Transfer calamari to serving platter and pour them over with mustard sauce and chopped parsley.

Grilled Shrimp in Spicy Lemon Butter

Prep time: 10 minutes | Cook time: 10 minutes | Serves 4

- 1½ pounds (680 g) shrimp, peeled and deveined
- 3 garlic cloves, minced
- 1 small onion, minced
- ½ cup butter
- 1½ tablespoons fresh parsley, chopped
- 1 tablespoon fresh lemon juice
- ¼ teaspoon red pepper flakes
- Pepper
- Salt

1. Preheat the griddle to high heat. 2. Melt butter on the griddle top. 3. Add garlic, onion, red chili flakes, pepper, and salt and stir for 2 minutes. 4. Season shrimp with pepper and salt and thread onto skewers. 5. Brush shrimp skewers with butter mixture. 6. Place shrimp skewers on griddle top and cook until shrimp turns to pink, about 3-4 minutes. 7. Transfer shrimp to the serving plate. 8. Drizzle lemon juice over shrimp and garnish with parsley. 9. Serve and enjoy.

Grilled Coconut-Pineapple Shrimp Skewers

Prep time: 1 hour 20 minutes | Cook time: 5 minutes | Serves 4

- 1½ pounds (680 g) uncooked jumbo shrimp, peeled and deveined
- ½ cup light coconut milk
- 1 tablespoon cilantro, chopped
- 4 teaspoons Tabasco Original Red Sauce
- 2 teaspoons soy sauce
- ¼ cup freshly squeezed orange juice
- ¼ cup freshly squeezed lime juice (from about 2 large limes)
- ¾ pounds (340 g) pineapple, cut into 1 inch chunks
- Olive oil, for griddleing

1. Combine the coconut milk, cilantro, Tabasco sauce, soy sauce, orange juice, lime juice. Add the shrimp and toss to coat. 2. Cover and place in the refrigerator to marinate for 1 hour. 3. Thread shrimp and pineapple onto metal skewers, alternating each. 4. Preheat griddle to medium heat. 5. Cook 5-6 minutes, flipping once, until shrimp turn opaque pink. 6. Serve immediately.

Grilled Salmon Steaks with Herbed Yogurt-Cilantro Drizzle

Prep time: 10 minutes | Cook time: 20 minutes | Serves 4

- Vegetable oil (for the griddle)
- 2 serrano chilis
- 2 garlic cloves
- 1 cup cilantro leaves
- ½ cup plain whole-milk Greek yogurt
- 1 tablespoon of extra virgin olive oil
- 1 teaspoon honey
- Kosher salt
- 2 (12 ounces / 340 g) bone-in salmon steaks
- Intolerances:
- Gluten-Free
- Egg-Free

1. Set up the griddle for medium-high heat, then oil the grate. 2. Expel and dispose of seeds from one chili. Mix the two chilis, garlic, cilantro, the yogurt, oil, the nectar, and ¼ cup water in a blender until it becomes smooth, then season well with salt. 3. Move half of the sauce to a little bowl and put it aside. Season the salmon steaks with salt. 4. Griddle it, turning more than once, until it's beginning to turn dark, about 4 minutes. 5. Keep on griddleing, turning frequently, and seasoning with residual sauce for at least 4 minutes longer.

White Wine and Parsley Marinated Trout

Prep time: 20 minutes | Cook time: 45 minutes | Serves 4

- ¼ cup olive oil
- 1 lemon juice
- ½ cup of white wine
- 2 cloves garlic minced
- 2 tablespoons fresh parsley, finely chopped
- Intolerances:
- Gluten-Free
- Egg-Free
- 1 teaspoon fresh basil, finely chopped
- Salt and freshly ground black pepper to taste
- 4 trout fish, cleaned
- Lemon slices for garnish
- Lactose-Free

1. In a large container, stir olive oil, lemon juice, wine, garlic, parsley, basil and salt and freshly ground black pepper to taste. 2. Submerge fish in sauce and toss to combine well. 3. Cover and marinate in refrigerate overnight. 4. When ready to cook, start the griddle on Smoke with the lid open for 4 to 5 minutes. Set the temperature to 400°F (205°C) and preheat, lid closed, for 10 to 15 minutes. 5. Remove the fish from marinade and pat dry on paper towel; reserve marinade. 6. Griddle trout for 5 minutes from both sides (be careful not to overcook the fish). 7. Pour fish with marinade and serve hot with lemon slices.

Chapter 3 Fish and Seafood

Grilled Prawn Skewers with Fresh Parsley

Prep time: 15 minutes | Cook time: 8 minutes | Serves 5

- ¼ cup fresh parsley leaves, minced
- 1 tablespoon garlic, crushed
- 2½ tablespoons olive oil
- 2 tablespoons Thai chili sauce
- 1 tablespoon fresh lime juice
- 1½ pounds (680 g) prawns, peeled and deveined

1. In a large bowl, add all ingredients except for prawns and mix well. 2. In a resealable plastic bag, add marinade and prawns. 3. Seal the bag and shake to coat well 4. Refrigerate for about 20-30 minutes. 5. Preheat the griddle to 450°F. 6. Remove the prawns from marinade and thread onto metal skewers. 7. Arrange the skewers onto the griddle and cook for about 4 minutes per side. 8. Remove the skewers from griddle and serve hot.

Spiced Jumbo Shrimp Skewers

Prep time: 15 minutes | Cook time: 8 minutes | Serves 6

- 1½ pounds (680 g) uncooked jumbo shrimp, peeled and deveined
- For the marinade:
- 2 tablespoons fresh parsley
- 1 bay leaf, dried
- 1 teaspoon chili powder
- 1 teaspoon garlic powder
- ¼ teaspoon cayenne pepper
- ¼ cup olive oil
- ¼ teaspoon salt
- ⅛ teaspoon pepper

1. Add marinade ingredients to a food processor and process until smooth. 2. Transfer marinade to a large mixing bowl. 3. Fold in shrimp and toss to coat; refrigerate, covered, 30 minutes. 4. Thread shrimp onto metal skewers. 5. Preheat griddle to medium heat. 6. Cook 5-6 minutes, flipping once, until shrimp turn opaque pink. 7. Serve immediately.

Asian-Spiced Seared Salmon

Prep time: 10 minutes | Cook time: 20 minutes | Serves 2

- 2 (4-ounce / 113g) salmon fillets
- ¾ cup Asian Griddle Sauce, plus more as needed
- cooking oil, as needed
- salt and pepper, to taste

1. Wash the salmon fillets and pat dry. Check for pin bones by placing salmon skin-side down on a cutting board and gently running your fingers across the thicker parts of the fillet. If you feel any bones, use a pair of tweezers to remove them before cooking. 2. Flip the salmon over, skin-side up. Typically, the salmon will resemble the shape of an airplane wing: thick, oval-round on one end, and tapering off to a very thin side on the other end. Make three or four ¼-inch cuts across the skin on the thickest part of the filet. This will allow the filet to cook a bit more evenly and with less curling when it is on the griddle. Season both sides of the filet with salt and pepper and make sure to get some seasoning into the areas where you scored the skin. 3. Bring the griddle grill to medium-high heat and add cooking oil to the surface. When the oil is shimmering, place the salmon skin-side down and cook for 3 or 4 minutes without disturbing. This develops a crispy crust on the salmon skin that many people find quite delicious. 4. When you are ready to flip, place the spatula on the griddle grill at an aggressive 15-degree angle and scrape under the skin to release and flip the salmon. 5. Shake the Asian Griddle Sauce well and add about ¾ cup to the griddle near the salmon. Slide the salmon into the sauce, cover it, and allow it to steam cook for another 5 minutes. If desired, flip the salmon an additional time and allow it to bathe in the Asian Griddle Sauce before plating.

Grilled Halibut Fillets in Spicy Rosemary Marinade

Prep time: 15 minutes | Cook time: 55 minutes | Serves 6

- 1 cup of virgin olive oil
- 2 large red chili peppers, chopped
- 2 cloves garlic, cut into quarters
- 1 bay leaf
- 1 twig of rosemary
- 2 lemons
- 4 tablespoon of white vinegar
- 4 halibut fillets
- Intolerances:
- Gluten-Free
- Egg-Free
- Lactose-Free

1. In a large container, mix olive oil, chopped red chili, garlic, bay leaf, rosemary, lemon juice and white vinegar. Submerge halibut fillets and toss to combine well. 2. Cover and marinate in the refrigerator for several hours or overnight. Remove anchovies from marinade and pat dry on paper towels for 30 minutes. 3. Start the griddle, set the temperature to medium and preheat, lid closed for 10 to 15 minutes. Griddle the anchovies, skin side down for about 10 minutes, or until the flesh of the fish becomes white (thinner cuts and fillets can cook in as little time as 6 minutes). 4. Turn once during cooking to avoid having the halibut fall apart. Transfer to a large serving platter, pour a little lemon juice over the fish, sprinkle with rosemary and serve.

Tuscan-Style Grilled Shrimp

Prep time: 10 minutes | Cook time: 5 minutes | Serves 4

- 1 pound (454 g) shrimp, deveined
- 1 teaspoon Italian seasoning
- 1 teaspoon paprika
- 1½ teaspoons garlic, minced
- 1 stick butter
- 1 fresh lemon juice
- ¼ teaspoon pepper
- ½ teaspoon salt

1. Preheat the griddle to high heat. 2. Melt butter on the hot griddle top. 3. Add garlic and cook for 30 seconds. 4. Toss shrimp with paprika, Italian seasoning, pepper, and salt. 5. Add shrimp into the pan and cook for 2-3 minutes per side. 6. Drizzle lemon juice over shrimp. 7. Stir and serve.

Grilled Fish with Fresh Salsa Verde

Prep time: 15 minutes | Cook time: 30 minutes | Serves 4

- 2 garlic cloves
- 3 tablespoons fresh orange juice
- 1 teaspoon dried oregano
- 2 cups of chopped white onion
- ¾ cup chopped cilantro
- ¼ cup extra virgin olive oil and more for the griddle
- 5 tablespoons fresh lime juice
- 1 pound (454 g) of tilapia, Intolerances:
- Gluten-Free
- striped bass or sturgeon fillets
- Kosher salt and grounded pepper
- 1 cup of mayonnaise
- 1 tablespoon of milk
- 4 corn tortillas
- 2 avocados, peeled and sliced
- ½ small head of cabbage, cored and thinly sliced
- Salsa Verde- Lime wedges
- Egg-Free

1. Mix the garlic, orange juice, oregano, one cup onion, ¼ cup cilantro, ¼ cup oil, and 3 tablespoon of lime juice in a medium bowl. 2. Season the fish with salt and grounded pepper.Spoon the ½ onion mixture on a glass baking dish then put the fish on it. 3. Spoon the remaining onion mixture over the fish and chill for half hour.Turn the fish , cover and chill for another half hour. 4. Mix the mayo, milk, and the remaining two tablespoon of lime juice in a little bowl. 5. Set up the griddle for medium-high heat and brush the grate with oil. 6. Griddle the fish, with some marinade on, till opaque in the center, about 3–5 minutes for each side. 7. Griddle the tortilla still slightly burned, about ten seconds per side. Coarsely chop the fish and put it onto a platter. 8. Serve with lime mayonnaise, tortillas, avocados, cabbage, Salsa Verde, lime wedges and the remaining cup of sliced onion and ½ cup cilantro.

Basil Pesto Grilled Shrimp

Prep time: 10 minutes | Cook time: 5 minutes | Serves 4

- 1 pound (454 g) shrimp, remove shells and tails
- ½ cup basil pesto
- Pepper
- Salt

1. Add shrimp, pesto, pepper, and salt into the large bowl and toss well.Set aside for 15 minutes. 2. Heat griddle over medium-high heat. 3. Thread marinated shrimp onto the skewers and place onto the hot griddle top and cook for 1-2 minutes on each side. 4. Serve and enjoy.

Savory Shrimp Skewers

Prep time: 10 minutes | Cook time: 7 minutes | Serves 6

- 1½ pounds (680 g) shrimp, peeled and deveined
- 1 tablespoon dried oregano
- 2 teaspoons garlic paste
- 2 lemon juice
- ¼ cup olive oil
- 1 teaspoon paprika
- Pepper
- Salt

1. Add all ingredients into the mixing bowl and mix well and place in the refrigerator for 1 hour. 2. Remove marinated shrimp from refrigerator and thread onto the skewers. 3. Preheat the griddle to high heat. 4. Place skewers onto the griddle top and cook for 5-7 minutes. 5. Serve and enjoy.

Cajun-Style Seared Salmon

Prep time: 10 minutes | Cook time: 10 minutes | Serves 5

- 1¼ pounds (567 g) salmon fillets
- 2 tablespoons blackened
- seasoning
- 2 tablespoons butter

1. Season salmon fillets with blackened seasoning. 2. Preheat the griddle to high heat. 3. Melt butter on the griddle top. 4. Place salmon fillets onto the hot griddle top and cook for 4-5 minutes. 5. Turn salmon and cook for 4-5 minutes more.Serve and enjoy.

Chapter 3 Fish and Seafood

Seared Scallops with Zesty Lemony Salsa Verde

Prep time: 15 minutes | Cook time: 15 minutes | Serves 2

- 2 tablespoons of vegetable oil and more for the griddle
- 12 large sea scallops, side muscle removed
- Kosher salt and grounded black pepper
- Lemony Salsa Verde
- Intolerances:
- Gluten-Free - Egg-Free - Lactose-Free

1. Set up the griddle for medium-high heat, then oil the grate. Toss the scallops with 2 tablespoons of oil on a rimmed baking sheet and season with salt and pepper. 2. Utilizing a fish spatula or your hands, place the scallops on the griddle. 3. Griddle them, occasionally turning, until gently singed and cooked through, around 2 minutes for each side. 4. Serve the scallops with Lemony Salsa Verde.

Seared Mahi-Mahi with Light Seasoning

Prep time: 10 minutes | Cook time: 10 minutes | Serves 4

- 4 (6 ounces / 170 g) mahi-mahi fillets
- 2 tablespoons olive oil
- Salt and ground black pepper, as required

1. Preheat the griddle to 350°F. 2. Coat fish fillets with olive oil and season with salt and black pepper evenly. 3. Place the fish fillets onto the griddle and cook for about 5 minutes per side. 4. Remove the fish fillets from griddle and serve hot.

Grilled Lobster Tails with Lime-Basil Butter

Prep time: 5 minutes | Cook time: 6 minutes | Serves 4

- 4 lobster tails (cut in half lengthwise)
- 3 tablespoons olive oil
- Lime wedges (to serve) - Sea salt, to taste
- For the lime basil butter:
- 1 stick unsalted butter, softened
- ½ bunch basil, roughly chopped
- 1 lime, zested and juiced
- 2 cloves garlic, minced
- ¼ teaspoon red pepper flakes

1. Add the butter ingredients to a mixing bowl and combine; set aside until ready to use. 2. Preheat griddle to medium-high heat. 3. Drizzle the lobster tail halves with olive oil and season with salt and pepper. 4. Place the lobster tails, flesh-side down, on the griddle. 5. Allow to cook until opaque, about 3 minutes, flip and cook another 3 minutes. 6. Add a dollop of the lime basil butter during the last minute of cooking .Serve immediately.

Open-Faced Clams with Spicy Horseradish Sauce

Prep time: 5 minutes | Cook time: 10 minutes | Serves 4

- 2 dozen littleneck clams, scrubbed
- 4 tablespoons unsalted butter, softened
- 2 tablespoons horseradish, drained
- 1 tablespoon hot sauce, like Tabasco
- ¼ teaspoon lemon zest, finely grated
- 1 tablespoon fresh lemon juice
- ¼ teaspoon smoked paprika
- Sea salt

1. Preheat the griddle to high. 2. Blend the butter with the horseradish, hot sauce, lemon zest, lemon juice, paprika, and pinch of salt. 3. Arrange the clams over high heat and griddle until they pop open, about 25 seconds. 4. Carefully turn the clams over using tongs, so the meat side is down. 5. Griddle for about 20 seconds longer, until the clam juices start to simmer. 6. Transfer the clams to a serving bowl. 7. Top each with about ½ teaspoon of the sauce and serve.

Crusted Blackened Tilapia

Prep time: 10 minutes | Cook time: 6 minutes | Serves 4

- 4 tilapia fillets
- 2 tablespoons butter
- 1 tablespoon olive oil
- For seasoning:
- 1½ teaspoons paprika
- 1 lemon, sliced
- ½ teaspoon ground cumin
- 1 teaspoon oregano
- ½ teaspoon garlic powder
- Pepper
- Salt

1. In a small bowl, mix together all seasoning ingredients and rub over fish fillets. 2. Preheat the griddle to high heat. 3. Add butter and oil on the hot griddle top. 4. Place fish fillets onto the griddle top and cook for 3 minutes. 5. Turn fish fillets and cook for 3 minutes more or until cooked through.Serve and enjoy.

Chapter 3 Fish and Seafood

Mediterranean-Style Salmon

Prep time: 10 minutes | Cook time: 6 minutes | Serves 2

- 12 ounces (340 g) salmon, cut into two pieces
- 1 teaspoon Greek seasoning
- 1 tablespoon olive oil
- ½ teaspoon lemon zest
- 1 garlic clove, minced
- Pepper - Salt

1. In a large bowl, mix olive oil, lemon zest, garlic, pepper, salt, and greek seasoning. 2. Add salmon in a bowl and coat well with marinade and set aside for 15 minutes. 3. Preheat the griddle to high heat. 4. Place marinated salmon on hot griddle top and cook for 2-3 minutes. Turn salmon to the other side and cook for 2-3 minutes more. 5. Serve and enjoy.

Zesty Lemon and Garlic Scallops

Prep time: 10 minutes | Cook time: 5 minutes | Serves 2

- 1 pound (454 g) frozen bay scallops, thawed, rinsed & pat dry
- 1 teaspoon garlic, minced
- 2 tablespoons olive oil
- 1 teaspoon parsley, chopped
- 1 teaspoon lemon juice
- Pepper
- Salt

1. Preheat the griddle to high heat. 2. Add oil to the griddle top. 3. Add garlic and sauté for 30 seconds. 4. Add scallops, lemon juice, pepper, and salt, and sauté until scallops turn opaque. 5. Garnish with parsley and serve.

Cod Fillets in Savory Onion Butter

Prep time: 10 minutes | Cook time: 15 minutes | Serves 4

- ¼ cupbutter
- 1 finely chopped small onion
- ¼ cupwhite wine
- 4 (6 ounces) cod fillets
Intolerances:
- Gluten-Free - Egg-Free
- 1 tablespoonof extra virgin olive oil
- ½ teaspoonsalt (or to taste)
- ½ teaspoonblack pepper
- Lemon wedges

1. Set up the griddle for medium-high heat. 2. In a little griddle liquefy the butter. Add the onion and cook for 1or2 minutes. 3. Add the white wine and let stew for an extra 3 minutes. Take away and let it cool for 5 minutes. 4. Spoon the fillets with extra virgin olive oil and sprinkle with salt and pepper. Put the fish on a well-oiled rack and cook for 8 minutes. 5. Season it with sauce and cautiously flip it over. Cook for 6 to 7 minutes more, turning more times or until the fish arrives at an inside temperature of 145°F (63°C). 6. Take away from the griddle, top with lemon wedges, and serve.

Trout with a Touch of Rosemary

Prep time: 10 minutes | Cook time: 5 hours | Serves 8

- 1 (7 pounds / 3.2 kg) whole lake trout, butterflied
- ½ cup kosher salt
- ½ cupfresh rosemary, chopped
- 2 teaspoons lemon zest, grated finely

1. Rub the trout with salt generously and then, sprinkle with rosemary and lemon zest. 2. Arrange the trout in a large baking dish and refrigerate for about 7-8 hours. 3. Remove the trout from baking dish and rinse under cold running water to remove the salt. 4. With paper towels, pat dry the trout completely. 5. Arrange a wire rack in a sheet pan. 6. Place the trout onto the wire rack, skin side down and refrigerate for about 24 hours. 7. Preheat the griddle to 180°F, using charcoal. 8. Place the trout onto the griddle and cook for about 2-4 hours or until desired doneness. 9. Remove the trout from griddle and place onto a cutting board for about 5 minutes before serving.

Squid in Citrus Soy Marinade

Prep time: 15 minutes | Cook time: 45 minutes | Serves 4

- 1 cup mirin
- 1 cup of soy sauce
- ⅓ cup yuzu juice or fresh lemon juice
Intolerances:
- Gluten-Free
- Egg-Free
- 2 cups of water
- 2 pounds (0.9 kg) squid tentacles left whole; bodies cut crosswise 1 inch thick
- Lactose-Free

1. In a bowl, mix the mirin, soy sauce, the yuzu juice, and water. 2. Put a bit of the marinade in a container and refrigerate it for later use. 3. Add the squid to the bowl with the rest of the marinade and let it sit for about 30 minutes or refrigerate for 4 hours. 4. Set up the griddle. Drain the squid. 5. Griddle over medium-high heat, turning once until white all through for 3 minutes. 6. Serve hot.

Seared Salmon Kebabs with Seasoned Rub

Prep time: 20 minutes | Cook time: 25 minutes | Serves 4

- 2 tablespoons of chopped fresh oregano
- 2 teaspoons of sesame seeds
- 1 teaspoon ground cumin
- 1 teaspoon Kosher salt
- ¼ teaspoon crushed red pepper flakes
- 1½ pounds (680 g) of skinless salmon fillets, cut into 1" pieces
- 2 lemons, thinly sliced into rounds
- 2 tablespoons of olive oil
- 16 bamboo skewerssoaked in water for one hour

Intolerances:
- Gluten-Free
- Egg-Free
- Lactose-Free

1. Set up the griddle for medium heat.Mix the oregano,sesame seeds, cumin,salt, and red pepper flakes in a little bowl.Put the spice blend aside. 2. String the salmon and the lemon slices onto 8 sets of parallel skewers in order to make 8 kebabs. 3. Spoon with oil and season with the spice blend. 4. Griddle and turn at times until the fish is cooked.

Grilled Shrimp with Polenta Cheese Cakes

Prep time: 8 minutes | Cook time: 30 minutes | Serves 4

- 3 cups water
- 1 tablespoon garlic salt
- 1 cup fine cornmeal/polenta
- 2 cups shredded white cheddar cheese, divided
- ¼ cup (½ stick) cold butter, divided
- 1 pound (454g) jumbo 21/25 shrimp, peeled and deveined
- White Wine Griddle Sauce, as needed
- cooking oil, as needed

1. Make the polenta cake in advance by bringing water and garlic salt to a boil in a medium pot over high heat. Reduce the heat to low, and add the polenta, stirring frequently to prevent clumping. Using a long-handled wooden spoon or heat-resistant spatula, stir constantly as you allow the polenta to cook at a very slow boil over low heat. Boiling polenta is extremely hot and unpleasant if it hits your skin, so take care to prevent it from splashing on you while cooking. Cook for 12 to 15 minutes, until it has thickened to a coarse pudding-like consistency, then stir in half the cheese and butter. Stirring frequently, allow the butter and cheese to melt completely, then add the remaining butter and cheese. Stir until fully melted. Carefully pour the polenta into a square baking pan or muffin tins, in a layer about an inch thick. Allow to cool 4 to 6 hours or overnight, covered in the refrigerator. 2. Bring the griddle grill to medium-high heat. Remove the polenta from the refrigerator and invert it onto a flat surface to take it out of the pan. If you used a baking pan, cut the polenta into squares based on how many servings you intend to make. 3. Grease the griddle grill well with cooking oil, and once it begins to shimmer, add the shrimp on one side and the polenta cakes on the other. Cover the shrimp and allow both the shrimp and the cakes to cook undisturbed for 3 to 4 minutes. 4. Flip all the shrimp and deglaze with some of the White Wine Griddle Sauce, then cover. To flip the polenta cakes, use a sturdy spatula, and scrape under the cake, making sure all the golden brown crust remains intact. The shrimp should be done when pink throughout and curled from head to tail, after about 6 minutes. 5. Serve the shrimp on top of the polenta cakes.

Chile-Lime Clams with Tomato and Flatbread

Prep time: 10 minutes | Cook time: 25 minutes | Serves 4

- 6 tablespoons unsalted pieces of butter
- 2 large shallots, chopped
- 4 thinly sliced garlic cloves
- 1 tablespoon of tomato paste
- 1 cup of beer
- 1 cup cherry tomatoes
- 1½ ounces (43 g) can-chickpeas, rinsed
- 2 tablespoons sambal oelek
- 24 scrubbed littleneck clams
- 1 tablespoon fresh lime juice
- 4 thick slices of country-style bread
- 2 tablespoons olive oil
- Kosher salt
- ½ cup cilantro leaves
- lime wedges

Intolerances:
- Gluten-Free
- Egg-Free

1. Set up the griddle for medium, indirect heat.Put a large griddle on the griddle over direct heat and melt 4 tablespoon of butter in it. 2. Add the shallots and garlic and keep cooking, often stirring, until they soften, about 4 minutes. 3. Add the tomato paste and keep cooking, continually stirring, until paste darkens to a rich brick red color.Add the beer and tomatoes. 4. Cook until the beer is reduced nearly by half, about 4 minutes.Add in the chickpeas and sambal oelek, then the clams. 5. Cover and keep cooking until clams have opened, maybe from 5 to 10 minutes depending on the size of clams and the heat.Discard any clams that don't open.Pour in the lime juice and the remaining 2 tablespoons of butter. 6. While griddling the clams, you can sprinkle the bread with oil and season with salt.Griddle until it becomes golden brown and crisp. 7. Put the toasts onto plates and spoon with clam mixture, then top with cilantro.Serve with lime wedges.

Grilled Salmon Fillet Skewers

Prep time: 10 minutes | Cook time: 10 minutes | Serves 4

- 1 pound (454 g) salmon fillets, cut into 1-inch cubes
- 2 tablespoons soy sauce
- 1 tablespoon toasted sesame seeds
- 1 lime zest
- 2 teaspoons olive oil
- 1½ tablespoon maple syrup
- 1 teaspoon ginger, crushed
- 1 lime juice

1. In a bowl, mix together olive oil, soy sauce, lime zest, lime juice, maple syrup, and ginger. 2. Add salmon and stir to coat. Set aside for 10 minutes. 3. Preheat the griddle to high heat. 4. Slide marinated salmon pieces onto the skewers and cook on a hot griddle top for 8-10 minutes or until cooked through. 5. Sprinkle salmon skewers with sesame seeds and serve.

Paprika-Garlic Seared Shrimp

Prep time: 10 minutes | Cook time: 5 minutes | Serves 4

- 1 pound (454 g) shrimp, peeled and cleaned
- 5 garlic cloves, chopped
- 2 tablespoons olive oil
- 1 tablespoon fresh parsley, chopped
- 1 teaspoon paprika
- 2 tablespoons butter
- ½ teaspoon sea salt

1. Add shrimp, 1 tablespoon oil, garlic, and salt in a large bowl and toss well and place in the refrigerator for 1 hour. 2. Preheat the griddle to high heat. 3. Add remaining oil and butter on the hot griddle top. 4. Once butter is melted then add marinated shrimp and paprika and stir constantly for 2-3 minutes or until shrimp is cooked. 5. Garnish with parsley and serve.

Fiery Grilled Squid

Prep time: 5 minutes | Cook time: 5 minutes | Serves 4

- 1½ pounds (680 g) Squid, red - Olive oil

For the marinade:

- 2 cloves garlic cloves, minced
- ½ teaspoon ginger, minced
- 3 tablespoons gochujang
- 3 tablespoons corn syrup
- 1 teaspoon yellow mustard
- 1 teaspoon soy sauce
- 2 teaspoons sesame oil
- 1 teaspoon sesame seeds
- 2 green onions, chopped

1. Preheat griddle to medium high heat and brush with olive oil. Add the squid and tentacles to the griddle and cook for 1 minute until the bottom looks firm and opaque.. Turn them over and cook for another minute; straighten out the body with tongs if it curls. Baste with sauce on top of the squid and cook 2 additional minutes. 2. Flip and baste the other side, cook 1 minute until the sauce evaporates and the squid turns red and shiny.

Seared Scallops Wrapped in Crispy Bacon

Prep time: 15 minutes | Cook time: 4 minutes | Serves 4

- 12 large sea scallops, side muscle removed
- 8 slices of bacon
- 1 tablespoon vegetable oil
- 12 toothpicks

1. Heat your griddle to medium heat and cook the bacon until fat has rendered but bacon is still flexible. Remove bacon from the griddle and place on paper towels. 2. Raise griddle heat to medium-high. 3. Wrap each scallop with a half slice of bacon and skewer with a toothpick to keep the bacon in place. 4. Place the scallops on the griddle and cook for 90 seconds per side. They should be lightly browned on both sides. 5. Remove from the griddle and serve immediately.

Lobster Tails with a Hint of Lemon

Prep time: 15 minutes | Cook time: 25 minutes | Serves 4

- ½ cup butter, melted
- 2 garlic cloves, minced
- 2 teaspoons fresh lemon juice
- Salt and ground black pepper, as required
- 4 (8 ounces / 227 g) lobster tails

1. Preheat the griddle to 450°F. 2. In a metal pan, add all ingredients except for lobster tails and mix well. 3. Place the pan onto the griddle and cook for about 10 minutes. 4. Meanwhile, cut down the top of the shell and expose lobster meat. 5. Remove pan of butter mixture from griddle. 6. Coat the lobster meat with butter mixture. 7. Place the lobster tails onto the griddle and cook for about 15 minutes, coating with butter mixture once halfway through. 8. Remove from the griddle and serve hot.

Seared Shrimp in Velvety Shrimp Butter

Prep time: 15 minutes | Cook time: 1 5 minutes | Serves 4

- 6 tablespoon unsalted butter
- ½ cup finely chopped red onion
- 1½ teaspoons crushed red pepper
- 1 teaspoon Malaysian shrimp paste
- 1½ teaspoons lime juice

Intolerances:

- Gluten-Free - Egg-Free
- salt
- grounded black pepper
- 24 shelled and deveined large shrimp
- 6 wooden skewers(better if soaked in water for 30 minutes)
- Torn mint leaves and assorted sprouts

1. In a little griddle, liquefy 3 tablespoon of butter. Add the onion then cook over moderate heat for about 3 minutes. 2. Add in the squashed red pepper and shrimp paste and cook until fragrant, about 2 minutes. 3. Add in the lime juice and the remaining 3 tablespoon of butter and season with salt. Keep the shrimp sauce warm. 4. Set up the griddle. Season the shrimp with salt and pepper and string onto the skewers, not too tightly. 5. Griddle over high heat, turning once until gently singed and cooked through, around 4 minutes. 6. Move onto a platter and spoon with shrimp sauce. Spread on the mint leaves and sprouts and serve.

Chapter 4
Beef, Pork, and Lamb

Chapter 4 Beef, Pork, and Lamb

Dijon and Paprika-Spiced Pork Tenderloin

Prep time: 10 minutes | Cook time: 4 hours | Serves 6

- 2 (1 pound / 454 g) pork tenderloins
- 2 tablespoons Dijon mustard
- 1½ teaspoons smoked paprika
- 1 teaspoon salt
- 2 tablespoons olive oil

1. Mix the mustard and paprika together in a small bowl until well combined. 2. Preheat the griddle to medium heat. 3. Rub the mustard mixture evenly over the tenderloins, ensuring they are fully coated. 4. Place the tenderloins on the hot griddle and cook, turning occasionally, until all sides are browned and the internal temperature reaches 135°F. 5. Take the tenderloins off the griddle and let them rest for 5 minutes. Slice and serve while warm. Enjoy!

Sweet and Savory Pineapple Bacon Chops

Prep time: 30 minutes | Cook time: 1 hour | Serves 6

- 1 large whole pineapple
- 6 pork chops

For the glaze:
- ¼ cup honey
- 12 slices thick-cut bacon
- Toothpicks, soaked in water
- ⅛ teaspoon cayenne pepper

1. Turn both burners to medium-high heat. After about 15 minutes, turn off one of the middle burners and reduce the remaining burners to medium heat. 2. Slice off the top and bottom of the pineapple, then peel it by cutting the skin off in strips. 3. Cut the pineapple flesh into six quarters. 4. Wrap each pineapple quarter with a slice of bacon and secure both ends with toothpicks. 5. Brush the pineapple quarters with honey and sprinkle with cayenne pepper. 6. Place the pineapple quarters on the griddle, turning them as needed to ensure the bacon cooks evenly on all sides. 7. While the pineapple is cooking, coat the pork chops with honey and cayenne pepper, then place them on the griddle. 8. Tent the pork chops loosely with foil and cook for 20 minutes. Flip the chops and continue cooking for another 10 to 20 minutes, or until they are fully cooked. 9. Serve each pork chop with a bacon-wrapped pineapple quarter on the side. Enjoy!

Spiced Mexican Beef Salad

Prep time: 10 minutes | Cook time: 10 minutes | Serves 2

Steak marinade:
- 2 tablespoons olive oil
- 3 garlic cloves, minced
- 2 teaspoons chili powder
- 1 teaspoon ground cumin
- 1 teaspoon kosher salt
- 1 teaspoon freshly ground pepper
- 1½ pounds (680 g) skirt or flap steak, cut into 4-inch lengths
- ½ cup lager beer

Salad:
- 12 ounces (340 g) romaine hearts, trimmed and chopped
- 1 can black beans, drained and rinsed
- 1 pint cherry tomatoes, halved
- 1 large ripe avocado, pitted, peeled, and cut into chunks
- About ⅓ cup crumbled queso fresco
- Chopped fresh cilantro, for garnish
- Kosher salt

Dressing:
- ½ cup plain whole milk yogurt
- ⅓ cup chopped fresh cilantro
- Zest of 1 lime
- Juice of 2 limes

1. Prepare the marinade and let the steak marinate for at least 4 hours or up to overnight. 2. In a large bowl, combine the salad ingredients and toss with the dressing until well mixed. Distribute the salad onto separate plates. Preheat the griddle to high heat, then place the marinated steak on the griddle. Reduce the heat to medium, tent the steak with foil, and cook for 5 minutes. 3. Flip the steak, tent it again, and cook for another 5 minutes. 4. Remove the steak from the griddle and slice it into 2-inch strips. 5. Arrange the steak strips on top of each individual salad, then sprinkle with flakey salt and a pinch of black pepper. Garnish with fresh cilantro and serve immediately. Enjoy!

Slow-Cooked Texas Beef Brisket

Prep time: 10 minutes | Cook time: 6 hour 20 minutes | Serves 6

- 1 (4½ pounds / 2.04 kg) flat cut beef brisket (about 3 inches thick)

For the rub:
- 1 tablespoon sea salt
- 1 tablespoon dark brown sugar
- 2 teaspoons smoked paprika
- 2 teaspoons chili powder
- 1 teaspoon garlic powder
- 1 teaspoon onion powder
- 1 teaspoon ground black pepper
- 1 teaspoon mesquite liquid smoke, like Colgin

1. In a small mixing bowl, combine all the rub ingredients. 2. Rinse the brisket under cold water, pat it dry with paper towels, and generously coat it with the coffee rub mixture. 3. Preheat the griddle for two-zone cooking: set one side to high heat and leave the other side on low heat. 4. Place the brisket on the high-heat side and sear for 3 to 5 minutes per side, until nicely charred. 5. Move the brisket to the low-heat side, tent it loosely with foil, and cook for 6 hours, or until a meat thermometer inserted into the thickest part reads 195°F. 6. Remove the brisket from the griddle and let it rest, covered, for 30 minutes to allow the juices to redistribute. 7. Slice the brisket thinly against the grain and serve. Enjoy!

Habanero-Infused Grilled Pork Chops

Prep time: 30 minutes | Cook time: 13 minutes | Serves 4

- 4½-inch-thick bone-in pork chops
- 3 tablespoons olive oil, plus

For the marinade:
- 1 habanero chili, seeded, chopped fine
- 2 garlic cloves, minced
- ½ cup fresh orange juice
- more for griddle
- Kosher salt and freshly ground black pepper
- 2 tablespoons brown sugar
- 1 tablespoon apple cider vinegar

1. In a large sealable plastic bag, combine all the marinade ingredients. 2. Pierce the pork chops with a fork to allow the marinade to penetrate, then place them in the bag. Seal the bag and turn it to ensure the pork chops are evenly coated. 3. Let the pork chops marinate at room temperature for 30 minutes, turning the bag occasionally. 4. Preheat the griddle to medium-high heat. 5. Lightly brush the griddle surface with oil. 6. Remove the pork chops from the marinade and pat them dry with paper towels to promote even searing. 7. Place the pork chops on the griddle and sear for about 8 minutes, turning occasionally, until they are charred on the outside and fully cooked. 8. Transfer the pork chops to a plate and let them rest for 5 minutes to retain their juices. 9. Serve the pork chops with your favorite side dishes and enjoy!

Marinated Beef Skewers

Prep time: 10 minutes | Cook time: 15 minutes | Serves 4

- 1 pound (454 g) beef sirloin tips

For marinade:
- ¼ cup olive oil
- 1 jalapeno pepper
- ½ tablespoon lime juice
- 1½ tablespoon red wine
- 1 zucchini, cut into chunks

- vinegar
- 1 teaspoon dried oregano
- 2 garlic cloves
- 1 cup cilantro

1. Add all the marinade ingredients to a blender and blend until smooth. 2. Pour the marinade into a mixing bowl, add the beef tips, and stir until the beef is well coated. Let the beef marinate for 30 minutes. 3. Thread the marinated beef tips and zucchini chunks alternately onto skewers. 4. Preheat the griddle to high heat. 5. Lightly spray the griddle surface with cooking spray. 6. Place the skewers on the hot griddle and cook for 7-8 minutes, turning occasionally, until the beef tips are fully cooked. 7. Serve immediately and enjoy!

Honey-Soy Glazed Pork Chop

Prep time: 1 hour | Cook time: 25 minutes | Serves 6

- 6 (4 ounce) boneless pork chops
- ¼ cup organic honey
- 1-2 tablespoons low sodium
- soy sauce
- 2 tablespoons olive oil
- 1 tablespoon rice mirin

1. In a bowl, combine honey, soy sauce, oil, and white vinegar. Whisk until the mixture is well blended. Place the pork chops and sauce into a large sealable plastic bag, seal it, and let the pork marinate for 1 hour. 2. Preheat the griddle to medium-high heat. Once hot, place the pork chops on the griddle and cook for 4 to 5 minutes, until the pork easily releases from the griddle surface. 3. Flip the pork chops and cook for another 5 minutes, or until the internal temperature reaches 145°F. 4. Remove from the griddle, serve immediately, and enjoy!

Chapter 4 Beef, Pork, and Lamb

Savory Dijon Beef Burger

Prep time: 10 minutes | Cook time: 10 minutes | Serves 4

- 1 pound (454 g) ground beef
- ½ teaspoon pepper
- ¾ tablespoon Worcestershire sauce
- 1 tablespoon Dijon mustard
- ⅛ teaspoon cayenne
- ⅛ teaspoon chili flakes
- 1 tablespoon parsley, chopped
- ½ teaspoon kosher salt

1. Place all the ingredients into a bowl and stir until everything is evenly combined. 2. Preheat the griddle to high heat. 3. Lightly coat the griddle surface with cooking spray. 4. Form the mixture into patties and place them on the hot griddle. Cook for 5 minutes on each side, or until fully cooked and golden brown. 5. Serve the patties hot and enjoy!

Simple and Tender Sirloin Steaks

Prep time: 10 minutes | Cook time: 15 minutes | Serves 4

- 4 top sirloin steaks
- 1 tablespoon Montreal steak seasoning
- Pepper
- Salt

1. Season the steaks generously with Montreal steak seasoning, pepper, and salt. 2. Preheat the griddle to medium heat. 3. Lightly spray the griddle surface with cooking spray. 4. Place the steaks on the hot griddle and cook for 3-5 minutes per side, or until the internal temperature reaches 145°F for medium doneness. 5. Serve the steaks immediately and enjoy!

Savory Sausage Grill Medley

Prep time: 5 minutes | Cook time: 22 minutes | Serves 4

- 8 mini bell peppers
- 2 heads radicchio, each cut into 6 wedges
- Canola oil, for brushing
- Sea salt
- Freshly ground black pepper
- 6 breakfast sausage links
- 6 hot or sweet Italian sausage links

1. Preheat the griddle to medium-high heat. 2. Brush the bell peppers and radicchio with oil, then season them with salt and black pepper. 3. Place the bell peppers and radicchio on the griddle and cook for 10 minutes without flipping. 4. While the vegetables are cooking, poke the sausages with a fork or knife and brush them with a bit of oil. 5. After 10 minutes, remove the vegetables from the griddle and set them aside. Lower the heat to medium and place the sausages on the griddle. Cook the sausages for 6 minutes. 6. Flip the sausages and cook for another 6 minutes, or until they are cooked through. Remove the sausages from the griddle. 7. Arrange the sausages and vegetables on a large cutting board or serving tray. Serve and enjoy!

Flank Steak Gyros with Greek Herbs

Prep time: 5 minutes | Cook time: 20 minutes | Serves 4

- 1 pound (454 g) flank steak
- 1 white onion, thinly sliced
- 1 roma tomato, thinly sliced
- 1 cucumber, peeled and thinly sliced
- ¼ cup crumbled feta cheese
- 6-inch pita pockets

For the marinade:

- ¼ cup olive oil, plus more for brushing
- 1 teaspoon dried oregano
- 1 teaspoon balsamic vinegar
- 1 teaspoon garlic powder
- Sea salt and freshly ground pepper, to taste

For the sauce:

- 1 cup plain yogurt
- 2 tablespoons fresh dill (can use dried), chopped
- 1 teaspoon garlic, minced
- 2 tablespoons lemon juice

1. Slice the flank steak into thin strips, making sure to cut against the grain. Place the marinade ingredients in a large sealable plastic bag, add the sliced meat, seal the bag, and turn it to ensure the meat is well coated. 2. Put the bag in the refrigerator and allow the meat to marinate for at least 2 hours, or overnight for best results. 3. Preheat the griddle to medium-high heat and set the oven to 250°F. 4. In a small mixing bowl, combine the sauce ingredients and set the bowl aside. 5. Lightly spritz the pitas with water, wrap them in foil, and warm them in the oven. 6. Brush the surface of the griddle with olive oil. 7. Add the marinated meat to the hot griddle, discarding any leftover marinade. Cook the meat for about 5 minutes, or until browned and cooked through. 8. Take the pitas out of the oven and cut them in half. 9. Place the pitas on serving plates and stuff them with cucumber, tomato, onion, and the cooked beef. Drizzle the yogurt sauce over the meat, sprinkle with feta cheese, and serve immediately. Enjoy!

Stuffed Beef Rolls with Buttered Noodles

Prep time: 15 minutes | Cook time: 1 hour | Serves 4

- 6 strips bacon
- 1 cup diced onion
- 1 pound (454g) thin cut sirloin tip or eye of round beef (about 8 slices)
- ½ cup yellow mustard
- 8 long thin dill pickle slices, cut into ribbons
- 16 ounces (454g) American-style lager
- 16 ounces (454g) beef stock
- 4 cups noodles, cooked and cooled
- ½ cup finely chopped fresh parsley, for garnish
- cooking oil, as needed
- salt and pepper, to taste

1. Preheat the griddle to medium-high heat. Cook the bacon for about 10 minutes until it's crispy. Let the bacon cool, crumble it into small pieces, and set aside. 2. Sauté the diced onion in the bacon grease on the griddle for about 5 minutes, until the onions become translucent. Scrape up any browned bits of bacon to incorporate extra flavor into the onions. Allow the onions to cool slightly. 3. To prepare the roulade, season both sides of a beef slice with salt and pepper. Place it on a cutting board, and if needed, trim the edges to form a rectangle. Spread a thin layer of mustard over the beef. Along one long edge, add about 2 tablespoons each of the crumbled bacon and sautéed onion, leaving a ¾-inch border clear. Lay ribbons of pickles on top of the bacon and onion mixture. 4. Starting from the edge with the filling, roll the beef tightly into a cigar shape, keeping it snug to prevent the filling from spilling out. Repeat this process with the remaining beef slices and fillings. 5. To cook the roulades, preheat the griddle to medium-high heat and add a bit of cooking oil. Once the oil shimmers, place the roulades seam side down on the griddle. Sear the seam side for 3 minutes to seal it, then roll the roulades, browning each side for 2 to 3 minutes until evenly browned. 6. For braising, place a skillet on the griddle. Arrange the roulades in a single layer inside the skillet. In a bowl, mix the lager and beef broth, then pour in enough liquid to cover about 80% of the roulades (if not using beer, double the beef broth). 7. Cover the skillet, leaving a small gap for steam to escape. Let the liquid reduce by half, about 15 to 20 minutes. Carefully rotate the roulades to submerge the unbraised portion, add another 1 to 2 cups of liquid, and cook for another 15 to 20 minutes until the meat is fork-tender. 8. While the roulades braise, melt butter on a clean section of the griddle. Add the noodles and cook, flipping with a spatula to brown and add texture. 9. To serve, place a bed of buttered noodles on each plate and top with two roulades. Drizzle the reduced braising liquid over the beef and noodles for extra flavor. Garnish with chopped parsley and serve immediately. Enjoy!

Perfectly Cooked NY Strip Steak

Prep time: 45 minutes | Cook time: 8 minutes | Serves 1

- 8 ounces (227 g) NY strip steak
- Olive oil - Sea salt
- Fresh ground black pepper

1. Take the steak out of the refrigerator and let it sit at room temperature for 30 to 45 minutes. 2. Preheat the griddle to medium-high heat and lightly brush the surface with olive oil. 3. Season the steak on all sides with salt and pepper. 4. Place the steak on the griddle and cook for 4 to 5 minutes. 5. Flip the steak and cook for another 4 minutes, or until it reaches an internal temperature of 125°F to 130°F for medium-rare. 6. Remove the steak from the griddle, place it on a plate, and let it rest for 5 minutes before serving. Enjoy!

Pork Tenderloin with a Mediterranean Herb Crust

Prep time: 2 hours | Cook time: 30 minutes | Serves 4

- 1 pound (454 g) pork tenderloin
- 1 tablespoon olive oil
- 2 teaspoons dried oregano
- ¾ teaspoon lemon pepper
- 1 teaspoon garlic powder
- ¼ cup parmesan cheese, grated
- 3 tablespoons olive tapenade

1. Place the pork tenderloin on a large piece of plastic wrap. 2. Rub the tenderloin with oil, then sprinkle evenly with oregano, garlic powder, and lemon pepper to coat the entire surface. 3. Wrap the tenderloin tightly in the plastic wrap and refrigerate for 2 hours to allow the flavors to infuse. 4. Preheat the griddle to medium-high heat. 5. Transfer the pork to a cutting board, remove the plastic wrap, and make a lengthwise cut down the center of the tenderloin, being careful not to cut all the way through, so the meat opens and lies flat. 6. In a small mixing bowl, combine the tapenade and parmesan. Spread the mixture into the center of the tenderloin, then fold the meat back together. 7. Secure the tenderloin by tying it with kitchen twine at 2-inch intervals. 8. Place the tenderloin on the griddle and sear for about 20 minutes, turning once, until the internal temperature reaches 145°F. 9. Move the tenderloin to a cutting board. 10. Tent it loosely with foil and let it rest for 10 minutes. 11. Remove the twine, slice the tenderloin into ¼-inch-thick pieces, and serve. Enjoy!

Cheese and Beef Patty Melt

Prep time: 8 minutes | Cook time: 18 minutes | Serves 2

- 2 cups sliced mushrooms
- 1 cup sliced sweet onions
- 2 (¼-pound / 113g) ground beef burger patties
- butter, as needed
- 4 slices deli rye or dark rye bread
- 4 slices Swiss cheese
- cooking oil, as needed
- salt and pepper, to taste

1. Preheat the griddle to medium-high heat. 2. Lightly coat the cooking surface with oil, then add the onions and mushrooms, keeping them in separate sections. Sprinkle both with salt and pepper. Sauté the mushrooms for 6 to 8 minutes, stirring and flipping frequently, until they shrink and develop a light brown color. The salt will help draw out moisture. Cook the onions until they are soft and slightly caramelized, about 5 minutes. Move the cooked mushrooms and onions to a cooler part of the griddle to keep them warm. 3. Season the burger patties with salt and pepper on both sides. Cook them on the griddle for 4 to 6 minutes per side, or until they reach your preferred doneness. Set the cooked burgers aside and keep warm. 4. To assemble the patty melts, spread butter on the griddle and place all four slices of bread onto the surface. Lay a slice of Swiss cheese on each slice of bread. Spoon the sautéed onion and mushroom mixture onto two of the bread slices. Place a cooked burger patty on top of each portion of onions and mushrooms. Finish with the remaining slices of bread, cheese side down. By now, the bread should be golden brown, and the cheese should be starting to melt. For extra crispiness and fully melted cheese, flip the assembled patty melts and let them cook a bit longer. Covering them for the final few minutes helps the cheese melt faster. Serve hot and enjoy!

Marinated Carne Asada Strips

Prep time: 1-2 hours | Cook time: 15 minutes | Serves 4

- 1 pound (454 g) hanger steak or shirt steak
- ¼ cup olive oil
- 1 lime, juiced
- 1 orange, juiced
- 1 garlic clove, finely chopped
- ½ teaspoon cumin
- ¼ teaspoon salt
- ¼ teaspoon ground pepper
- handful of fresh cilantro, chopped

1. Place all the ingredients into a large sealable plastic bag and mix well to ensure the contents are evenly coated. Let the meat marinate in the refrigerator for 1 to 2 hours. 2. Preheat the griddle to medium-high heat. Once hot, cook the meat for 3 minutes per side, or until it is just cooked through. 3. Remove the meat from the griddle and transfer it to a cutting board. Let it rest for 10 minutes to allow the juices to redistribute. 4. Slice the meat against the grain and serve immediately. Enjoy!

Espresso-Crusted Skirt Steak

Prep time: 10 minutes | Cook time: 20 minutes | Serves 8

- ¼ cup coffee beans, finely ground
- ¼ cup dark brown sugar, firmly packed - ½ teaspoon sea salt
- ⅛ teaspoon ground cinnamon
- Pinch cayenne pepper
- ½ pound (227 g) skirt steak, cut into 4 pieces
- 1 tablespoon olive oil

1. Preheat the griddle to high heat. 2. In a bowl, mix together the coffee, brown sugar, salt, cinnamon, and cayenne pepper to create the spice rub. 3. Take the steak out of the refrigerator and let it sit at room temperature for about 15 minutes. Rub the steak with oil, then generously coat it with the spice rub, massaging it into the meat to ensure it sticks well. 4. Sear the steak on the hot griddle for 2 to 4 minutes per side, until it develops a charred crust and reaches medium-rare doneness. 5. Transfer the steak to a cutting board, cover it loosely with foil, and let it rest for 5 minutes. Finally, thinly slice the steak against the grain and serve. Enjoy!

Fiery Cajun Pork Cutlets

Prep time: 10 minutes | Cook time: 15 minutes | Serves 4

- 4 pork chops
- 1 tablespoon paprika
- ½ teaspoon ground cumin
- ½ teaspoon dried sage
- ½ teaspoon salt
- ½ teaspoon black pepper
- ½ teaspoon garlic powder
- ¼ teaspoon cayenne pepper
- 1 tablespoon butter
- 1 tablespoon vegetable oil

1. In a medium bowl, mix together the paprika, cumin, sage, salt, pepper, garlic, and cayenne pepper until well combined. 2. Preheat the griddle to medium-high heat, then add the butter and oil, letting them melt and heat up. 3. Generously rub the pork chops with the seasoning mixture, ensuring they are evenly coated. 4. Place the pork chops on the hot griddle and cook for 4 to 5 minutes. Flip the pork chops and cook for an additional 4 minutes, or until they are cooked through. 5. Remove the pork chops from the griddle and let them rest for 5 minutes before serving. Enjoy!

Chapter 4 Beef, Pork, and Lamb

Spiced Pork Tenderloin with Harissa Cream Sauce

Prep time: 40 minutes | Cook time: 20 minutes | Serves 6

- 2 (1 pound / 454 g) pork tenderloins
- 1 teaspoon ground cinnamon
- 1 teaspoon ground cilantro

For Creamy Harissa Sauce:
- 1 cup Greek yogurt (8 ounces / 227 g)
- 1 tablespoon fresh lemon juice
- 1 tablespoon extra-virgin olive oil
- 1 teaspoon ground cumin
- 1 teaspoon paprika
- 1 teaspoon sea salt
- 2 tablespoons olive oil

- 1 teaspoon harissa sauce
- 1 clove garlic, minced
- Kosher salt and cracked black pepper

1. In a small mixing bowl, combine all the harissa ingredients and set the mixture aside. 2. In another bowl, mix together the cinnamon, coriander, cumin, paprika, salt, and olive oil until it forms a paste. 3. Rub the seasoning mixture evenly over the pork tenderloins, ensuring they are well coated. Cover and refrigerate for 30 minutes to let the flavors develop. 4. Preheat the griddle to high heat. Once hot, place the tenderloins on the griddle and cook for 8 to 10 minutes, until nicely browned. 5. Flip the tenderloins and cook for another 8 to 10 minutes. Transfer them to a cutting board, tent with foil, and let them rest for 10 minutes. 6. Slice the tenderloins and serve with the creamy harissa sauce. Enjoy!

Pork Shoulder in Peach Mojo Sauce

Prep time: 1 hour | Cook time: 6 minutes | Serves 12

- 1 (6 pounds / 2.7 kg) pork shoulder
- 1 quart Hawaiian Mojo
- ½ cup sea-salt
- 1 can peach slices, in syrup
- 2 tablespoon garlic powder
- 2 tablespoon red pepper flakes
- 15 ounces (425 g) sliced peaches in syrup
- 16 ounces (453 g) peach preserves
- 12 ounces (340 g) apricot & pineapple preserves
- ½ cup Stubbs Mesquite Liquid Smoke

1. Inject the pork shoulder with mojo marinade, making sure it penetrates deeply. Let it marinate overnight in the refrigerator. Before roasting, allow the pork to sit at room temperature. Smoke the pork shoulder for 5 to 6 hours, or until the internal temperature reaches 185°F. 2. Once cooked, slice the pork and layer the pieces in a pan. Generously slather the top with peach-pineapple glaze. Place the pan under a hot broiler for 5 to 10 minutes until the glaze is caramelized and browned. 3. Serve the tender pork with sweet Hawaiian rolls and fluffy white rice. Enjoy!

Classic Roast Beef Sandwich

Prep time: 10 minutes | Cook time: 5 minutes | Serves 1

- 2 bread slices
- 2 cheese slices
- 4 deli roast beef, sliced
- 2 teaspoons butter
- 1 tablespoon mayonnaise
- ¼ cup caramelized onions, sliced

1. Butter one side of each bread slice evenly. 2. On the unbuttered side of one bread slice, spread mayonnaise, then layer with beef, onions, and cheese. 3. Place the second slice of bread on top, buttered side facing out. 4. Preheat the griddle to high heat. 5. Lightly coat the griddle surface with cooking spray. 6. Put the sandwich on the hot griddle and cook for about 5 minutes, flipping halfway through, until both sides are golden brown and the cheese is melted. 7. Remove from the griddle, serve immediately, and enjoy!

Filet Mignon with Caprese Topping

Prep time: 10 minutes | Cook time: 10 minutes | Serves 4

- 6 ounces filets
- 2 teaspoons garlic salt
- Italian Olive oil
- 2 roma tomatoes, sliced
- 2 ounces (57 g) fresh buffalo mozzarella, cut into four slices
- 8 fresh basil leaves
- Balsamic vinegar glaze, for drizzling
- Sea salt, for seasoning
- Fresh ground pepper

1. Lightly brush all sides of each filet with olive oil and season with garlic salt. Preheat the griddle to high heat. Once hot, place the steaks on the griddle, reduce the heat to medium, tent loosely with foil, and cook for 5 minutes. 2. Flip the steaks, re-tent with foil, and cook for another 5 minutes. During the last 2 minutes of cooking, top each steak with a slice of mozzarella cheese and allow it to melt. 3. Remove the steaks from the griddle and top each with a few slices of tomato and 2 fresh basil leaves. Drizzle with balsamic glaze, sprinkle with sea salt and black pepper, and serve immediately. Enjoy!

Tender Buttermilk Pork Roast

Prep time: 20 minutes | Cook time: 3 hours | Serves 4-6

- 1 (3 to 3½-pounds / 1.36 kg to 1.6 kg) pork sirloin roast

1. Trim all the fat and silver skin from the pork roast. 2. Place the pork roast into a 1-gallon sealable plastic bag or brining container with the buttermilk brine. 3. Refrigerate overnight, turning the roast periodically if possible. 4. Remove the pork sirloin roast from the brine and pat it dry with a paper towel. 5. Insert a meat probe into the thickest part of the roast. 6. Set up the griddle for indirect cooking and preheat it to 225°F. 7. Smoke the roast for 3 to 3½ hours, or until the internal temperature reaches 145°F. 8. Let the roast rest under a loose tent of foil for 15 minutes, then slice against the grain. Enjoy!

Speedy Marinade Skirt Steak

Prep time: 30 minutes | Cook time: 45 minutes | Serves 4

- 2 (8 ounce) skirt steaks

For the marinade:
- 2 tablespoons balsamic vinegar
- 2 teaspoons olive oil, more for brushing
- 2 garlic cloves, minced
- Sea salt, to taste
- Black pepper, to taste

1. In a sealable plastic bag, combine all the marinade ingredients. Add the steaks, seal the bag, and turn it to ensure the steaks are well coated. Let them marinate at room temperature for 30 minutes. 2. Preheat the griddle to medium-high heat. 3. Remove the steaks from the marinade and discard the marinade. Place the steaks on the griddle and cook for about 3 minutes per side. 4. Transfer the steaks to a cutting board and let them rest for 5 minutes. 5. Slice the steaks against the grain and serve with your favorite sides. Enjoy!

Smashed Patty Burgers

Prep time: 6 minutes | Cook time: 10 minutes | Serves 4

- 4 burger buns
- 1 pound (454g) ground chuck (80/20), divided into 4-ounce (113g) balls
- 4 slices American cheese
- salt and pepper, to taste

1. Preheat the griddle to high heat. Cut 4 squares of parchment paper. Butter the griddle surface, then toast the inside of the burger buns for 1 to 2 minutes, until they are golden brown and warmed through. Set the buns aside. 2. Scrape the griddle clean with a spatula or scraper. Place the ground beef balls on the griddle, spacing them 6 to 8 inches apart. Put a parchment paper square over one beef ball and press it down with a bacon press, flattening it to about ¼ inch thick. Remove the parchment paper and repeat with the remaining beef balls. Season the exposed sides of the burgers generously with salt and pepper. 3. Let the smashed burgers cook for about 2 minutes undisturbed. Use a heavy-duty spatula to scrape underneath each burger, making sure to get all the browned bits, and flip them. Repeat for the remaining burgers. 4. Place a slice of cheese on each burger and let it cook for another 2 minutes, or until the cheese starts to melt. For extra melty cheese, cover the burgers briefly while they finish cooking. 5. Using the spatula, scrape under each burger at a sharp angle to release them from the griddle and place them onto the toasted burger buns. 6. Add toppings like lettuce, tomato, onion, and your favorite condiments if desired, or simply enjoy the rich, meaty flavor of the burger with the buttery toasted bun. Serve immediately and enjoy!

Yucatan-Spiced Pork on the Griddle

Prep time: 15 minutes | Cook time: 8 minutes | Serves 4

ngredients:
- 2 pork tenderloins, trimmed
- 1 teaspoon annatto powder
- Olive oil

For the marinade:
- 2 oranges, juiced
- 2 lemons, juiced, or more to taste
- 2 limes, juiced, or more to taste
- 6 cloves garlic, minced
- 1 teaspoon ground cumin
- ½ teaspoon cayenne pepper
- ½ teaspoon dried oregano
- ½ teaspoon black pepper

1. Combine the marinade ingredients in a mixing bowl and whisk until well blended. 2. Cut the tenderloins in half crosswise, then cut each piece in half lengthwise. 3. Place the pork pieces in the marinade, making sure they are thoroughly coated. 4. Cover with plastic wrap and refrigerate for 4 to 6 hours. 5. Remove the pork from the marinade and transfer to a paper-towel-lined bowl to absorb excess moisture. 6. Discard the paper towels, then drizzle olive oil and a bit more annatto powder over the pork pieces. 7. Preheat the griddle to medium-high heat and lightly oil the surface. 8. Place the pork pieces on the griddle, spacing them evenly, and cook for 4 to 5 minutes. 9. Flip the pieces and cook for another 4 to 5 minutes on the other side. 10. Transfer the pork to a serving platter and let it rest for about 5 minutes before serving. Enjoy!

Bell Peppers Stuffed with Eggs and Crispy Bacon

Prep time: 10 minutes | Cook time: 15 minutes | Serves 4

- 1 cup shredded Cheddar cheese
- 4 slices bacon, cooked and chopped
- 4 bell peppers, seeded and tops removed
- 4 large eggs
- Sea salt
- Freshly ground black pepper
- Chopped fresh parsley, for garnish

1. Begin by preheating the griddle to medium-high heat. 2. Distribute the cheese and bacon evenly among the bell peppers, then carefully crack an egg into each pepper and season with salt and pepper. 3. Position each bell pepper on the griddle and cook for approximately 10 to 15 minutes, or until the egg whites are set but the yolks remain slightly runny. 4. Finally, take the peppers off the griddle, sprinkle them with parsley as a garnish, and serve them hot.

New York-Style Chopped Beef and Cheese

Prep time: 15 minutes | Cook time:10 minutes | Serves 3

- 1 pound (454g) ground beef
- 1 small onion, minced
- 1 tablespoon onion powder
- 1 tablespoon garlic powder
- 1 tablespoon pepper
- 1 teaspoon salt
- 9 slices American cheese
- 3 hero rolls, or other similar bread
- butter or cooking oil, as needed
- Toppings
- lettuce
- tomato
- ketchup
- mayonnaise
- pickles
- mushrooms
- bell peppers
- jalapenos
- marinara sauce
- Thousand Island dressing
- breaded mozzarella sticks

1. Bring the griddle to medium heat and coat the surface with butter or your preferred cooking oil. Place the meat on one side of the griddle and the onion on another part, allowing the onions to sauté until they turn translucent. 2. While the meat is cooking, use a spatula or scraper to chop it into small pieces. Season with onion powder, garlic powder, pepper, and salt. Continue chopping and cooking until the meat changes color from red to pink, then to brown. 3. Once the meat is chopped and just cooked through, mix in the sautéed onions. Divide the mixture into three equal portions, then top each portion with three slices of cheese spread evenly. Cover to help the cheese melt faster. 4. Scoop up each portion of the meat and cheese mixture and serve on bread. For an extra burst of flavor, add any combination of your favorite toppings. Enjoy!

Pork Chops Topped with Herbed Apple Relish

Prep time: 5 minutes | Cook time: 20 minutes | Serves 4

- 4, bone-in pork chops
- 2 honeycrisp apples, peeled, cored and chopped
- ⅓ cup orange juice
- 1 teaspoon chopped fresh rosemary
- 1 teaspoon chopped fresh sage
- Sea salt
- Black pepper

1. Start by combining the apples, herbs, and orange juice in a saucepan and simmer over medium heat until the apples are soft and the liquid has reduced to a syrupy consistency, about 10 to 12 minutes. 2. Season the pork chops with salt and pepper. 3. Cook the chops on the griddle until they can be easily lifted off, about 4 minutes on each side. 4. Flip the chops carefully and cook for another 3 minutes on the opposite side. 5. Remove the chops from the griddle and place them on a cutting board, covering them with foil to rest. 6. Serve the chops topped with the apple compote.

Pineapple-Glazed Beef Burger

Prep time: 10 minutes | Cook time: 8 minutes | Serves 4

- 1¼ pounds (567 g) ground beef
- 2 pineapple slices, chopped
- ¼ teaspoon pepper
- 1 garlic clove, minced
- 1 teaspoon ginger, grated
- ¼ cup green onions, chopped
- ¼ cup soy sauce
- Salt

1. Place all the ingredients in a bowl and stir thoroughly until everything is evenly combined. 2. Heat the griddle to high heat. 3. Lightly coat the griddle surface with cooking spray to prevent sticking. 4. Form the mixture into patties and place them on the hot griddle. Cook for about 4 minutes per side, flipping once, until they are golden brown and fully cooked through. 5. Remove the patties from the griddle, serve immediately, and enjoy your meal!

Ribeye Pork Loin Florentine Style

Prep time: 30 minutes | Cook time: 1 hour | Serves 6

- 1 (3 pounds / 1.36 kg) boneless ribeye pork loin roast
- 4 tablespoons extra-virgin olive oil, divided
- 2 tablespoons Pork Dry Rub or your favorite pork seasoning
- 4 bacon slices
- 6 cups fresh spinach
- 1 small red onion, diced
- 6 cloves garlic, cut into thin slivers
- ¾ cup shredded mozzarella cheese

1. Trim away any abundance fat and silver skin. 2. Butterfly the pork loin or approach your butcher to butterfly it for you. There are numerous phenomenal recordings online with nitty gritty directions on the various systems for butterflying a loin roast. 3. Rub 2 tablespoons of the olive oil on each side of the butterflied roast and season the two sides with the rub. 4. Cook the bacon in a large griddle over medium heat. Disintegrate and set aside. Reserve the bacon fat. 5. Griddle the pork loin for 60 to 75 minutes, or until the internal temperature at the thickest part arrives at 140°F. 6. Rest the pork loin under a free foil tent for 15 minutes before cutting contrary to what would be expected.

Rustic Tuscan Steak and Golden Potatoes

Prep time: 30 minutes | Cook time: 35 minutes | Serves 4

- 2 bone-in porterhouse steaks
- 1½ pounds (680 g) small potatoes, like Yukon Gold, scrubbed but skins left on, halved
- 3 tablespoons extra-virgin olive oil, divided
- Sea salt and freshly ground pepper, to taste
- 2 teaspoons red wine, like Sangiovese or Montepulciano
- 1 teaspoon balsamic vinegar
- pinch red pepper flakes
- 2 fresh rosemary sprigs, needles removed (discard stems)

1. Add the potatoes to a large pot, cover with water, and bring to a boil over high heat. Reduce the heat to medium-high and cook until the potatoes are almost tender, about 10 minutes. Drain the potatoes, transfer them to a medium mixing bowl, coat with 2 tablespoons of olive oil, and set aside. Preheat the griddle to medium heat. In a separate bowl, whisk together 2 tablespoons of olive oil, rosemary, red wine vinegar, and red pepper flakes. Add the steaks to the marinade and set aside until ready to cook. 2. Season the potatoes with salt and pepper. 3. Place the steaks on one side of the griddle and the potatoes on the other side. 4. Cook the steaks for 5 minutes, then flip and cook for another 4 minutes for medium-rare doneness. 5. Let the potatoes cook on the griddle for 5 minutes, stirring occasionally for even browning. 6. Transfer the steaks to a cutting board, tent with aluminum foil, and let them rest for 5 minutes while the potatoes finish cooking. 7. Cut each steak into 2 pieces and distribute them among 4 dinner plates. Add the potatoes around the steaks and serve hot. Enjoy!

Vietnamese Ground Pork Banh Mi

Prep time: 8 minutes | Cook time: 10 minutes | Serves 4

- ¼ cup rice wine vinegar
- 3 tablespoons sugar
- 1 cup carrot matchsticks
- ¼ cup mayonnaise
- ½ cup minced cilantro, divided
- 1 tablespoon sriracha
- 1 pound (454g) ground pork shoulder
- ¼ cup grated onion
- 1 clove garlic, minced
- 3 tablespoons soy sauce
- 2 tablespoons fish sauce
- 1 teaspoon salt, divided
- 1 teaspoon pepper
- 4 French bread–style sandwich buns
- cilantro sprigs, for garnish

1. In a microwave-safe bowl, heat the rice wine vinegar, sugar, and ½ teaspoon salt until the sugar and salt dissolve, about 45 seconds. Pour the warm vinegar mixture over the carrot matchsticks in a medium bowl and place in the refrigerator to cool. In a small bowl, combine the mayonnaise, 1 tablespoon of minced cilantro, and sriracha. Set aside and keep chilled. 2. In a large bowl, mix the ground pork with the remaining minced cilantro, onion, garlic, soy sauce, fish sauce, the remaining salt, and pepper. Cover and refrigerate for at least 1 hour or up to overnight to let the flavors meld. 3. Preheat the griddle to medium-high heat. Add the pork mixture to the griddle and sauté, chopping it with a spatula for about 5 minutes. Cover and cook for an additional 4 to 6 minutes, adding a little water to the griddle to help with steaming. 4. Slice the sandwich buns in half and toast them on the griddle until lightly browned and warmed through. Spread the cilantro-sriracha mayonnaise on one side of each bun. Place a quarter of the cooked pork onto each bun and top with the pickled carrots and fresh cilantro sprigs. Serve immediately and enjoy!

Roast Beef and Tomato Sandwich

Prep time: 10 minutes | Cook time: 10 minutes | Serves 2

- 4 bread slices
- ½ pound (227 g) deli roast beef slices
- 2 tablespoons mayonnaise
- 1 tablespoon butter
- ½ onion, sliced
- 1 tomato, sliced
- 4 cheese slices

1. Spread butter on one side of each bread slice. 2. Take 4 slices of bread and spread the unbuttered sides with mayonnaise. Layer each with beef, cheese, tomatoes, and onions. 3. Top with the remaining bread slices, buttered side facing out. 4. Preheat the griddle to high heat. 5. Lightly coat the griddle surface with cooking spray. 6. Place the sandwiches on the hot griddle and cook for about 5 minutes, flipping once, until both sides are golden brown. 7. Serve the sandwiches warm and enjoy!

Loaded Bacon Monster Burgers

Prep time: 10 minutes | Cook time:20 minutes | Serves 2

- 2 large sesame-seed burger buns
- 6 strips bacon
- 1 tablespoon salt
- 1 tablespoon pepper
- 1 tablespoon onion powder
- 1 tablespoon garlic powder
- 2 (⅓-pound / 150g) burger patties
- 4 slices cheese (optional)
- butter, as needed
- Toppings
- mayonnaise
- mustard
- ketchup
- lettuce
- 1 medium, firm tomato, cut into thick slices
- 1 medium, sweet onion, cut into rings
- dill pickle chips

1. Preheat the griddle to medium-high heat. Add butter to the surface, letting it melt, and toast the sesame-seeded buns for 2 to 3 minutes, until they are golden brown and warmed. Set the buns aside. 2. Place the bacon on the griddle and cook for 6 to 8 minutes, or until it reaches your preferred level of crispiness. Remove the bacon and keep it warm. 3. In a small bowl, mix together the salt, pepper, onion powder, and garlic powder. Season both sides of the burger patties with the seasoning mix. Place the patties on the griddle where the bacon was cooked and cover. Cook for 4 to 5 minutes, until red juices appear on the surface of the patties. Flip the patties, add cheese if desired, and cover. Cook for another 2 to 3 minutes, or until the burgers reach your desired doneness. For medium-rare, aim for an internal temperature of 135°F, checking with an instant-read thermometer. 4. To assemble the burger, spread mayonnaise on the bottom bun. Place the patty with melted cheese on top, followed by the bacon and any toppings you like. Finish with the top bun and enjoy your burger!

Chapter 5
Pizzas, Wraps, and Sandwiches

Chapter 5 Pizzas, Wraps, and Sandwiches

Bacon Jalapeno Wraps

Prep time: 5 minutes | Cook time: 10 minutes | Serves 4

- package bacon, uncured and nitrate free
- fresh jalapeno peppers, halved lengthwise and seeded
- 1 (8 ounce) package cream cheese
- 1 dozen toothpicks, soaked

1. Preheat your griddle to high heat. 2. Fill jalapeno halves with cream cheese. 3. Wrap each with bacon. Secure with a toothpick. 4. Place on the griddle, and cook until bacon is crispy, about 5 to 7 minutes per side. 5. Remove to a platter to cool and serve warm.

Veggie Pesto Flatbread

Prep time: 40 minutes | Cook time: 10 minutes | Serves 4

- 2 flatbreads
- jar pesto
- cup shredded mozzarella cheese
- For the topping:
- ½ cup cherry tomatoes, halved
- 1 small red onion, sliced thin
- 1 red bell pepper, sliced
- 1 yellow bell pepper, sliced
- ½ cup mixed black and green olives, halved
- 1 small yellow squash or zucchini, sliced
- teaspoon olive oil
- ¼ teaspoon sea salt
- ¼ teaspoon black pepper

1. Preheat the griddle to low heat. 2. Spread an even amount of pesto onto each flatbread. 3. Top with ½ cup mozzarella cheese each. 4. Mix all the topping ingredients together in a large mixing bowl with a rubber spatula. 5. Lay flatbreads on griddle, and top with an even amount of topping mixture; spreading to the edges of each. 6. Tent the flatbreads with foil for 5 minutes each, or until cheese is just melted. 7. Place flatbreads on a flat surface or cutting board, and cut each with a pizza cutter or kitchen scissors. 8. Serve warm!

Spiced Lamb Burger

Prep time: 5 minutes | Cook time: 5 minutes | Serves 4

- 1¼ pounds (567 g) lean ground lamb
- tablespoon ground cumin
- ¼ teaspoon ground cinnamon
- ½ teaspoon salt
- ½ teaspoon freshly ground black pepper
- whole wheat pitas
- ½ medium cucumber, peeled and sliced
- ½ cup Simple Garlic Yogurt Sauce

1. Put the lamb in a medium bowl with the cumin, cinnamon, salt, and pepper. Using a fork, mix the seasonings into the meat and then, with your hands, form the mixture into 4 patties, each about 1 inch thick. 2. Turn control knob to the high position, when the griddle is hot place the burgers and cook for 5 minutes without flipping. Remove the burgers and cover to keep warm. Put a burger into each pita, stuff a few cucumber slices in there too, and spoon some of the yogurt sauce over the top. Serve immediately.

Ultimate Grilled Cheese

Prep time: 10 minutes | Cook time: 10 minutes | Serves 4

- 8 slices sourdough bread
- 4 slices provolone cheese
- 4 slices yellow American cheese
- 4 slices sharp cheddar cheese
- 4 slices tomato
- 3 tablespoons mayonnaise
- 3 tablespoons butter

1. Heat your griddle to medium heat. 2. Butter one side of each piece of bread and spread mayo on the other side. 3. Place the buttered side down on the griddle and stack the cheeses on top. 4. Place the other pieces of bread, butter side up on top of the cheese and cook until golden brown. Flip and cook until the other piece of bread is golden brown as well and the cheese is melted. 5. Remove from the griddle, slice in half and enjoy.

Griddle Vegetable Pizza

Prep time: 30 minutes | Cook time: 10 minutes | Serves 6

- 8 small fresh mushrooms, halved
- 1 small zucchini, cut into ¼-inch slices
- 1 small yellow pepper, sliced
- 1 small red pepper, sliced
- 1 small red onion, sliced
- 1 tablespoon white wine vinegar
- 1 tablespoon water
- 4 teaspoons olive oil, divided
- ½ teaspoon dried basil
- ¼ teaspoon sea salt
- ¼ teaspoon pepper
- 1 prebaked, 12-inch thin whole wheat pizza crust
- 1 can (8 ounces / 227 g) pizza sauce
- 1 small tomatoes, chopped
- 2 cups shredded part-skim mozzarella cheese

1. Preheat your griddle to medium-high heat. 2. Combine mushrooms, zucchini, peppers, onion, vinegar, water, 3 teaspoons oil and seasonings in a large mixing bowl. 3. Transfer to griddle and cook over medium heat for 10 minutes or until tender, stirring often. 4. Brush crust with remaining oil and spread with pizza sauce. 5. Top evenly with Griddle vegetables, tomatoes and cheese. 6. Tent with aluminum foil and griddle over medium heat for 5 to 7minutes or until edges are lightly browned and cheese is melted. 7. Serve warm!

Pineapple Teriyaki Turkey Burgers

Prep time: 5 minutes | Cook time: 9 minutes | Serves 4

- 1 teaspoon BBQ rub
- 1 can sliced pineapple
- 4 slices Swiss cheese

patry:

- 1 pound (454 g) ground turkey
- ½ cup bread crumbs
- ¼ cup teriyaki sauce
- 1 small yellow onion, diced
- 1 cup fresh raw spinach, stems removed
- 4 sets of hamburger buns
- 2 tablespoons finely chopped parsley
- 2 cloves garlic, minced
- 1 egg, beaten

1. In a large mixing bowl, combine all patty ingredients and mix thoroughly by hand. 2. Divide mixture into four equal parts.Form the four portions into patties and lay on parchment paper.Sprinkle each patty evenly with BBQ rub.Place in refrigerator for 30 minutes. 3. Bring the griddle to high heat.When the griddle is hot, place the burgers and pineapple slices.Cook for 4 minutes without flipping.Remove the burgers and cover to keep warm. 4. After burgers are flipped over, add a slice of Swiss cheese to each patty and allow to melt as patty finishes cooking.Remove from griddle. 5. Layer burgers on buns with spinach and pineapple.

Triple-Decker Monte Cristo Sandwich

Prep time: 10 minutes | Cook time:15 minutes | Serves 2

- 3 ounces (85g) Black Forest deli ham
- 3 ounces (85g) smoked deli turkey
- 3 slices thick-sliced bread or Texas toast
- 2 slices Swiss cheese
- 2 slices American cheese
- 2 tablespoons mayonnaise, divided
- 1 cup Buttermilk Pancake batter, plus 2 tablespoons water
- powdered sugar, for dusting
- ¼ cup warm maple syrup, to serve
- ¼ cup raspberry jam, to serve
- cooking oil, as needed
- butter, as needed

1. Bring the griddle grill to medium-high heat. 2. Melt a little butter on the grill and cook the ham and turkey slices for 3 to 4 minutes, or until the meat is slightly caramelized and takes on some color. 3. Remove the crusts from the bread. Add half the mayonnaise to a slice of bread, then add the Swiss cheese, and then the ham. Cover with a second slice of bread. Add the turkey slices, then the American cheese. Coat the third slice of bread with the remaining mayonnaise and put it face-down on the top of the sandwich. 4. Place a large piece of plastic wrap on a flat surface. Put the sandwich in the middle of the plastic wrap. Fold the plastic wrap over the sandwich and press down firmly on it to compress and push some air out of the bread. Wrap the sandwich tightly by rolling it forward to the edge of the plastic wrap and tuck the ends over the top to secure. Allow the sandwich to rest in the refrigerator for 2 to 6 hours. 5. Bring the griddle to medium heat. Oil the griddle well. 6. Lightly dredge the sandwich in the pancake batter and place on the griddle. Cook each side for 3 to 5 minutes, covered. When each of the sides has lightly browned, use tongs and cook the edges of the sandwich for 45 to 60 seconds per edge. The pancake batter should form a nice crust, but you should also see evidence of the cheese melting inside the sandwich. 7. Traditionally, the Monte Cristo sandwich is cut into triangles and served with a dusting of powdered sugar. Having warm maple syrup and raspberry jam on hand for dipping only sweetens the deal.

Turkey And Melted Brie Sandwich With Green Chiles

Prep time: 5 minutes | Cook time: 10 minutes | Serves 1

- 3 tablespoons roasted, diced green chiles
- 6 ounces (170g) sliced deli turkey
- 2 slices thick-sliced bread
- 4 ounces (113g) Brie, thinly sliced
- butter, as needed

1. Bring the griddle grill to medium heat. 2. Melt butter on the griddle and sauté the green chiles for about 3 minutes, to warm them and add a little caramelization. 3. Add more butter to the grilling surface and fan out the turkey slices on the griddle to warm them and get a slightly browned color. Cook for 2 to 3 minutes per side. 4. Butter the griddle again and place the two slices of bread on the griddle. Lay half of the sliced Brie on each of the slices of bread to allow the Brie to warm. Place half of the warmed turkey slices on top of the Brie on each slice of bread and allow the warm turkey to assist in melting the cheese. Add the warmed chiles to one slice of bread and use the other slice to cover the chiles, making a sandwich. 5. Cover and allow the sandwich to continue to cook for about 4 minutes, flipping once, until the cheese is fully melted. The sandwich will be very hot and gooey with the melted cheese, so consider allowing it to rest for about 4 minutes before eating—if you can resist.

Big Burger

Prep time: 5 minutes | Cook time: 9 minutes | Serves 4

- 1¼ pounds (567 g) lean ground beef
- ½ teaspoon salt
- ½ teaspoon freshly ground black pepper
- Seasoning of your choice (such as a dash of Worcestershire or hot sauce, or 1 teaspoon Spicy Spanish Rub
- 4 slices cheese such as American, cheddar, or Swiss (about 4 ounces / 113 g), or ¼ cup
- crumbled blue or goat cheese
- 4 toasted buns
- 4 beefsteak tomato slices
- 4 leaves romaine lettuce

1. Bring the griddle to medium-high heat. Put the beef in a medium bowl and add the salt, pepper, and your preferred seasonings. 2. Using a fork, mix the seasonings into the meat and then, with your hands, form the mixture into 4 patties, each about 1 inch thick. When the griddle is hot, place the burgers on the Griddle and cook for 4 minutes without flipping. 3. Cooking is complete when the internal temperature of the beef reaches at least 145°F on a food thermometer. If needed, cook for up to 5 more minutes. 4. Lay the cheese over the burgers and lower the griddle. Griddle for 30 seconds, just until the cheese melts. 5. Set the burgers onto the bottom halves of the buns, add a slice of tomato and a leaf of lettuce to each burger, and cover with the tops of the buns. Serve immediately.

Mini Portobello Burgers

Prep time: 15 minutes | Cook time: 15 minutes | Serves 4

- portobello mushroom caps
- slices mozzarella cheese

For the marinade:

- ¼ cup balsamic vinegar
- 2 tablespoons olive oil
- teaspoon dried basil
- 1 teaspoon dried oregano
- 4 buns, like brioche
- 1 teaspoon garlic powder
- ¼ teaspoon sea salt
- ¼ teaspoon black pepper

1. Whisk together marinade ingredients in a large mixing bowl. Add mushroom caps and toss to coat. 2. Let stand at room temperature for 15 minutes, turning twice. 3. Preheat griddle for medium-high heat. 4. Place mushrooms on the griddle; reserve marinade for basting. 5. Cook for 5 to 8 minutes on each side, or until tender. 6. Brush with marinade frequently. 7. Top with mozzarella cheese during the last 2 minutes of cooking. 8. Remove from griddle and serve on brioche buns.

Turkey Burger

Prep time: 5 minutes | Cook time: 4 minutes | Serves 4

- 1 pound (454 g) ground turkey
- cup pine nuts or walnut pieces
- tablespoons grated Parmesan cheese
- tablespoons store-bought pesto
- ¼ teaspoon salt
- ¼ teaspoon freshly ground black pepper
- whole wheat pitas
- romaine lettuce leaves or 1 small handful arugula
- Lemon

1. Preheat the griddle to high. 2. Put the turkey in a medium bowl and add the pine nuts, Parmesan, pesto, salt, and pepper. Using a fork, mix the seasonings into the meat and then, with your hands, form the mixture into 4 patties, each about 1 inch thick. 3. Griddle the patties for about 4 minutes, until they have taken on griddle marks and are cooked through. Put each burger into a pita with some lettuce and a squeeze of lemon juice. Serve immediately.

Chapter 5 Pizzas, Wraps, and Sandwiches

Chipotle Burgers With Avocado

Prep time: 5 minutes | Cook time: 5 minutes | Serves 4

- 1¼ pounds (567 g) lean ground beef
- 2 tablespoons chipotle puree
- ½ teaspoon salt
- ¼ teaspoon freshly ground black pepper
- slices cheddar cheese (about 4 ounces / 113 g)
- 1 avocado, halved, pitted, and sliced
- ¼ head iceberg lettuce, shredded
- 4 hamburger buns, toasted

1. Put the beef in a medium bowl and add the chipotle puree, salt, and pepper. Using a fork, mix the seasonings into the meat and then, with your hands, form the mixture into 4 patties, each about 1 inch thick. 2. Turn control knob to the high position, when the griddle is hot, place the burgers and cook for 4 minutes without flipping. Topping each burger with a slice of cheese and cook for 1 minute more, until the cheese melts. Remove the burgers and cover to keep warm. 3. Top each burger with a few slices of avocado and some shredded lettuce before sandwiching between a bun. 4. Chipotle Puree: Put canned chipotles and their liquid in a blender or food processor and process until smooth. 5. The puree can be covered with plastic wrap and refrigerated for up to 2 weeks. This stuff is hot-hot-hot, so a little goes a long way. I use it in meat marinades and dips. The puree is sold in some grocery stores, in ethnic mark.

New Mexican Salsa Verde

Prep time: 5 minutes | Cook time: 15 minutes | Serves 1 cup

- cloves garlic (leave the skins on),
- skewered on a wooden toothpick or small bamboo skewer
- 1 cup roasted New Mexican green chiles or Anaheim chiles cut into ¼-inch strips (8 to 10 chiles
- 2 tablespoons chopped fresh
- cilantro
- 2 teaspoons fresh lime juice, or more to
- taste
- ½ teaspoon ground cumin
- ½ teaspoon dried oregano
- Coarse salt (kosher or sea) and freshly
- ground black pepper

1. Preheat the griddle to high. When ready to cook, lightly oil the griddle surface. Place the burgers on the hot griddle. The burgers will be done after cooking 4 to 6 minutes. Put the garlic cloves until they are lightly browned and tender, 2 to 3 minutes per side (4 to 6 minutes in all). Scrape any really burnt skin off the garlic. Place the garlic, chile strips, cilantro, lime juice, cumin, oregano, and 4 tablespoons of water in a blender and purée until smooth, scraping down the sides of the blender with a spatula. 2. Transfer the salsa to a saucepan and bring to a gentle simmer over medium heat. Let simmer until thick and flavorful, 5 to 8 minutes, stirring with a wooden spoon. The salsa should be thick (roughly the consistency of heavy cream) but pourable; add more water as needed. Taste for seasoning, adding more lime juice as necessary and salt and pepper to taste; the salsa should be highly seasoned.

Griddle Pizza Cheese

Prep time: 10 minutes | Cook time: 20 minutes | Serves 4

- 8 slices French bread
- 3 tablespoons butter, softened
- ½ cup pizza sauce
- ¼ cup mozzarella cheese
- ½ cup pepperoni diced
- Garlic powder, for dusting
- Oregano, for dusting

1. Spread butter on one side of each French bread slice. 2. Place butter side down on a piece of aluminum foil and dust with garlic powder and oregano. 3. Spread pizza sauce on opposite side of all French bread slices. 4. Top 4 slices of bread with mozzarella cheese, a few slices of pepperoni, and additional mozzarella. 5. Place remaining French bread slices on top of pizza topped bread, butter side up, to create 4 sandwiches. 6. Preheat the griddle to medium heat and place one slice of bread, buttered side down into the griddle. 7. Cook, 3 minutes and flip to cook 3 minutes on the other side; cook until bread is golden and cheese is melted. 8. Serve warm and enjoy!

Garlicky Pork Burgers

Prep time: 5 minutes | Cook time: 10 minutes | Serves 4

- 1 teaspoon salt
- 1 teaspoon black pepper
- 4 cloves garlic, chopped
- 4 hard rolls, split, or 8–10 slider buns

1. Put the meat, salt, pepper, and garlic in a food processor and pulse until coarsely ground—finer than chopped, but not much. (If using preground meat, put it in a bowl with the salt, pepper, and garlic and work them together gently with your hands.) 2. Handling the meat as little as possible to avoid compressing it, shape it lightly into 4 burgers, 1 to 1½ inches thick. (You can do this several hours in advance; cover with plastic wrap and refrigerate until you're ready to griddle.) 3. Turn control knob to the high position, when the griddle is hot, place the burgers on and cook for 10 minutes without flipping; the internal temperature should be 160°F (check with an instant-read thermometer, or nick with a small knife and peek inside). 4. Transfer to a platter. 5. Toast the rolls. Serve the burgers on the rolls.

Grilled Vegetable Pizza

Prep time: 30 minutes | Cook time: 10 minutes | Serves 6

- 8 small fresh mushrooms, halved
- 1 small zucchini, cut into ¼-inch slices
- 1 small yellow pepper, sliced
- 1 small red pepper, sliced
- 1 small red onion, sliced
- 1 tablespoon white wine vinegar
- 1 tablespoon water
- 4 teaspoons olive oil, divided
- ½ teaspoon dried basil
- ¼ teaspoon sea salt
- ¼ teaspoon pepper
- 1 prebaked, 12-inch thin whole wheat pizza crust
- 1 can (8 ounces / 227 g) pizza sauce
- 2 small tomatoes, chopped
- 2 cups shredded part-skim mozzarella cheese

1. Preheat your griddle to medium-high heat. 2. Combine mushrooms, zucchini, peppers, onion, vinegar, water, 3 teaspoons oil and seasonings in a large mixing bowl. 3. Transfer to griddle and cook over medium heat for 10 minutes or until tender, stirring often. 4. Brush crust with remaining oil and spread with pizza sauce. 5. Top evenly with grilled vegetables, tomatoes and cheese. 6. Tent with aluminum foil and griddle over medium heat for 5 to 7 minutes or until edges are lightly browned and cheese is melted. 7. Serve warm!

Basil-Ginger Shrimp Burgers

Prep time: 5 minutes | Cook time: 10 minutes | Serves 4

- large clove garlic, peeled
- 1 1-inch piece fresh ginger, peeled and sliced
- 1½ pounds (680 g) shrimp, peeled (and deveined if you like)
- ½cup lightly packed fresh basil leaves
- ¼cup roughly chopped shallots, scallions, or red onion
- Salt and pepper
- Sesame oil for brushing the burgers
- sesame hamburger buns or 8–10 slider buns
- Lime wedges for serving
- Lettuce, sliced tomato, and other condiments for serving (optional)

1. Put the garlic, ginger, and one-third of the shrimp in a food processor; purée until smooth, stopping the machine to scrape down the sides as necessary.Add the remaining shrimp, the basil, and shallots, season with salt and pepper, and pulse to chop.Form into 4 burgers about ¾ inch thick (or 8 to 10 sliders).Transfer to a plate, cover with plastic wrap, and chill until firm, at least 1 or up to 8hours. 2. Turn control knob to the high position, when the griddle is hot, brush the burgers on both sides with oil then put them on the griddle-and cook until the bottoms brown and they release easily, 5 to 7minutes.Carefully turn and cook until opaque all the way through, 3 to 5minutes. 3. Put the buns, cut side down, on the griddle to toast.Serve the burgers on the toasted buns with lime wedges, as is or dressed however you like.

Tzatziki Lamb Burgers

Prep time:5 minutes | Cook time: 12 minutes | Serves 5

- 1½ pounds (680 g) boneless lamb shoulder or leg or good-quality ground lamb
- 1 tablespoon chopped fresh oregano
- 1 teaspoon salt
- 1 teaspoon black pepper
- 1 tablespoon minced garlic
- ½cup Greek yogurt
- 1 tablespoon olive oil, plus more for brushing
- 1 tablespoon red wine vinegar
- 2 tablespoons crumbled feta cheese
- 4 or 5 ciabatta rolls, split, or 8–10 slider buns (like potato or dinner rolls)
- Thinly sliced cucumbers for serving

1. Put the lamb, oregano, salt, pepper, and garlic in a food processor and pulse until coarsely ground—finer than chopped, but not much.(If you're using preground meat, put it in a bowl with the seasonings and work them together gently with your hands.) 2. Take a bit of the mixture and fry it up to taste for seasoning; adjust if necessary. 3. Handling the meat as little as possible to avoid compressing it, shape the mixture lightly into 4 or 5 burgers or 8 to 10 sliders. 4. Refrigerate the burgers until you're ready to griddle; if you make them several hours in advance, cover with plastic wrap. 5. Whisk the yogurt, oil, and vinegar together in a small bowl until smooth.Stir in the feta.Taste and adjust the seasoning with salt and pepper. 6. Bring the griddle to high heat.When the griddle is hot, place the burgers and cook for 11 minutes. 7. Transfer the burgers to a plate.Brush the cut sides of the rolls lightly with oil and toast directly over the griddle, 1 to 2minutes.Top with a burger, then several slices of cucumber, a dollop of the sauce, and the other half of the roll.Serve with the remaining sauce on the side.

Tex-Mex Turkey Burgers

Prep time: 10 minutes | Cook time: 15 minutes | Serves 4

- ⅓ cup finely crushed corn tortilla chips
- 1 egg, beaten
- ¼ cup salsa
- ⅓ cup shredded pepper Jack cheese
- Pinch salt
- Freshly ground black pepper
- 1 pound (454 g) ground turkey
- 1 tablespoon olive oil
- 1 teaspoon paprika

1. In a medium bowl, combine the tortilla chips, egg, salsa, cheese, salt, and pepper, and mix well. 2. Add the turkey and mix gently but thoroughly with clean hands. 3. Form the meat mixture into patties about ½ inch thick. Make an indentation in the center of each patty with your thumb so the burgers don't puff up while cooking. 4. Brush the patties on both sides with the olive oil and sprinkle with paprika. 5. Griddle. Turn control knob to the high position. When the griddle is hot, griddle for 14 to 16 minutes or until the meat registers at least 165°F.

Salmon Burgers

Prep time: 5 minutes | Cook time: 11 minutes | Serves 4

- 1½ pounds (680 g) salmon fillet, skin and any remaining pin bones removed, cut into chunks
- 2 teaspoons Dijon mustard
- 3 scallions, trimmed and chopped
- ¼ cup bread crumbs (preferably fresh)
- Salt and pepper
- Good-quality olive oil for brushing
- sesame hamburger buns or 8–10 slider buns (like potato or dinner rolls)
- 1 large tomato, cut into 4 thick slices

1. Put about one quarter of the salmon and the mustard in a food processor and purée into a paste. Add the rest of the salmon and pulse until chopped. Transfer to a bowl, add the scallions, bread crumbs, and a sprinkle of salt and pepper. Mix gently just enough to combine. Form into 4 burgers ¾ to 1 inch thick. Transfer to a plate, cover with plastic wrap, and chill until firm, at least 2 or up to 8 hours. 2. Turn control knob to the high position, when the griddle is hot, brush the burgers with oil on both sides, then put them on the griddle. Cook for 11 minutes. 3. After 11 minutes, check the burgers for doneness. Cooking is complete when the internal temperature reaches at least 165°F on a food thermometer. 4. If necessary, close the hood and continue cooking for up to 2 minutes more. 5. Remove the burgers from the griddle. Put the buns on the griddle, cut side down, and toast for 1 to 2 minutes. Serve the burgers on the buns, topped with the tomato if using.

Chapter 6
Vegetables and Sides

Chapter 6 Vegetables and Sides

Smoked Jalapeño Poppers

Prep time: 15 minutes | Cook time: 60 minutes | Serves 4 to 6

- 12 medium jalapeños
- 6 slices bacon, cut in half
- 8 ounces (227 g) cream cheese, softened
- 1 cup cheese, grated
- 2 tablespoons pork & poultry rub

1. When you're ready to start cooking, adjust the temperature to 180°F and preheat the griddle with the lid closed for 15 minutes. 2. Halve the jalapeños lengthwise and use a small spoon or paring knife to remove the seeds and ribs. 3. Combine softened cream cheese with a Pork & Poultry rub and grated cheese until well mixed. 4. Place a spoonful of this mixture onto each jalapeño half, wrap it with a strip of bacon, and fasten it with a toothpick. 5. Arrange the jalapeños on a rimmed baking sheet and place them on the griddle to smoke-cook for 30 minutes. 6. Afterward, increase the griddle's temperature to 375°F and cook for an additional 30 minutes or until the bacon reaches your desired level of doneness. Serve these jalapeño poppers warm and enjoy!

Sticky Caramel Smoked Onion

Prep time: 30 minutes | Cook time: 1hour | Serves 10

- 2½ pounds (1.1 kg) onions
- ½ cup salted butter
- 3 tablespoons brown sugar
- 1 tablespoon molasses
- 2 tablespoons apple cider vinegar
- 1 tablespoon worcestershire sauce
- 2 teaspoons dry mustard
- 1 teaspoon smoked paprika
- 1 teaspoon onion powder

1. Begin by peeling the onions and slicing them into rings, then arrange them in a disposable aluminum pan. 2. Combine brown sugar, molasses, apple cider vinegar, Worcestershire sauce, dry mustard, smoked paprika, and onion powder in a bowl, and sprinkle this spice mix over the sliced onions, shaking the pan to ensure they're evenly coated. 3. Add a few pats of butter on top of the onions and set the pan aside. 4. Configure the griddle for indirect heat and adjust the temperature to 225°F(107 degrees Celsius). 5. Place the aluminum pan with onions in the griddle and smoke cook for an hour and a half, or until the spice mixture has caramelized beautifully. 6. After the onions are ready, remove the pan from the griddle and transfer the smoked onions to a serving dish, gently stirring them a little. 7. Serve the onions warm and enjoy the flavors.

Griddle Sugar Snap Peas

Prep time: 15 minutes | Cook time: 10 minutes | Serves 4

- 2 pounds (0.9 kg) sugar snap peas, ends trimmed
- ½ teaspoon garlic powder
- 1 teaspoon salt
- ⅔ teaspoon ground black pepper
- 2 tablespoons olive oil

1. Turn on the griddle or set it to 450 and let it preheat for at least 15 minutes. 2. As the griddle heats up, prepare a medium bowl with peas, garlic powder, oil, salt, and black pepper, tossing them until they're well mixed, then spread them on a sheet pan. 3. When the griddle is preheated, open the lid, place the sheet pan on the griddle grate, close the griddle, and smoke cook for 10 minutes until the peas show slight charring. 4. Serve the peas hot right away.

Lemon-Garlic Artichokes

Prep time: 10 minutes | Cook time: 15 minutes | Serves 4

- Juice of ½ lemon
- ½ cup canola oil
- 3 garlic cloves, chopped - Sea salt
- Freshly ground black pepper
- 2 large artichokes, trimmed and halved

1. Start by preheating the griddle to medium-high heat. 2. As the griddle heats, mix lemon juice, oil, and garlic in a medium bowl, season with salt and pepper, and then use this lemon-garlic blend to brush over the cut sides of the artichoke halves. 3. Arrange the artichokes on the grill with their cut sides facing down, press down gently to ensure even grill marks, and cook for 8 to 10 minutes, regularly basting them with the lemon-garlic mixture until they're blistered on all sides.

Blistered Green Beans

Prep time: 5 minutes | Cook time: 10 minutes | Serves 4

- 1 pound (454 g) haricots verts or green beans, trimmed
- 2 tablespoons vegetable oil
- Juice of 1 lemon
- Pinch red pepper flakes
- Flaky sea salt
- Freshly ground black pepper

1. Start by preheating the griddle to medium-high heat. As the griddle heats up, place green beans in a medium bowl and toss them with oil until they are evenly coated. 2. Transfer the green beans to the grill and cook for 8 to 10 minutes, stirring frequently until they are blistered on all sides. Once cooked, arrange the green beans on a large serving platter, squeeze lemon juice over them, sprinkle with red pepper flakes, and season with sea salt and black pepper to taste.

Smoked Healthy Cabbage

Prep time: 10 minutes | Cook time: 2 hours | Serves 4

- 1 head cabbage, cored
- 4 tablespoons butter
- 2 tablespoons rendered bacon fat
- 1 chicken bouillon cube
- 1 teaspoon fresh ground black pepper
- 1 garlic clove, minced

1. Begin by preheating your griddle to 240°F. 2. Fill the cavity of your cored cabbage with a mixture of butter, a bouillon cube, bacon fat, pepper, and minced garlic. 3. Wrap the cabbage in aluminum foil, covering about two-thirds of its height. 4. Ensure that the top of the cabbage remains open to allow steam to escape. 5. Place the wrapped cabbage on the griddle rack and smoke cook for 2 hours. 6. After the cabbage has finished cooking, unwrap it and serve immediately for a delicious meal.

Corn & Cheese Chile Rellenos

Prep time: 30 minutes | Cook time: 65 minutes | Serves 4

- 2 pounds (0.9 kg) Ripe tomatoes, chopped
- 4 cloves garlic, chopped
- ½ cup sweet onion, chopped
- 1 jalapeno, stemmed, seeded, and chopped
- 8 large green new Mexican or poblano chiles
- 3 ears sweet corn, husked
- ½ teaspoon Dry oregano, Mexican, crumbled
- 1 teaspoon Ground cumin
- 1 teaspoon Mild chile powder
- ⅛ teaspoon Ground cinnamon
- Salt and freshly ground pepper
- 3 cups grated Monterey jack
- ½ cup Mexican crema
- 1 cup queso fresco, crumbled
- Fresh cilantro leaves

1. Arrange tomatoes, garlic, onion, and jalapeño in a shallow baking dish and position it on the griddle to cook. 2. Once the tomato mixture has cooled, transfer it to a blender and blend until smooth, then pour it into a saucepan. 3. Stir in cumin, oregano, chile powder, cinnamon, and season with salt and pepper to taste. 4. Gently peel the blistered skin off the New Mexican chiles, ensuring to keep the stem ends intact and avoiding tearing the flesh. 5. Remove the corn kernels from the cobs and place them in a large mixing bowl. 6. Bake the rellenos for 25 to 30 minutes, or until the filling is bubbling and the cheese has melted. 7. Finally, sprinkle with queso fresco and garnish with fresh cilantro leaves, if desired, before enjoying.

Radish Browns With Black Beans And Red Peppers

Prep time: 6 minutes | Cook time: 10 minutes | Serves 4

- 1 bunch radishes, cleaned and grated
- ½ cup diced red bell pepper
- 2 cloves garlic, minced
- ½ cup cooked black beans, drained
- 1 teaspoon garlic powder
- 1 teaspoon onion powder
- sour cream, to serve
- coconut oil or other cooking oil, as needed
- salt and pepper, to taste

1. As your griddle grill preheats to medium, trim the tops and bottoms from the radishes, rinse them thoroughly under cold water, and clean them well. The fastest method to grate the radishes is using a food processor; however, if you don't have one, a handheld grater will yield the same results. 2. Apply a generous amount of oil to the griddle surface. Once the oil starts to glisten, add diced red pepper and minced garlic, and sauté for approximately 2 minutes until they soften. 3. Incorporate the shredded radishes, black beans, garlic powder, and onion powder into the pan, season with salt and pepper, and shape the mixture into a cake about half an inch thick. Cover the griddle and let the radishes cook for 4 to 5 minutes, or until they start to develop a golden hue. 4. Add a bit more oil to the griddle, and when it's hot, flip the radish cake into the fresh oil. Cook for an additional 3 to 4 minutes on the other side until it's also browned. Serve the radish cake with a dollop of sour cream, if desired.

Stir Fry Bok Choy

Prep time: 10 minutes | Cook time: 5 minutes | Serves 4

- 2 heads bok choy, trimmed and cut crosswise
- 1 teaspoon sesame oil
- 2 teaspoons soy sauce
- 2 tablespoons water
- 1 tablespoon butter
- 1 tablespoon peanut oil
- 1 tablespoon oyster sauce
- ½ teaspoon salt

1. Begin by combining soy sauce, oyster sauce, sesame oil, and water in a small bowl, then set this marinade aside. 2. Preheat the griddle to high heat. 3. Once hot, add oil to the griddle surface. 4. Toss in the bok choy along with a pinch of salt and stir-fry for approximately 2 minutes. 5. Incorporate the butter and the reserved soy sauce mixture into the pan, continuing to stir-fry for an additional 1 to 2 minutes. 6. Finally, serve the dish hot and enjoy the flavors.

Home Fries With Veggies

Prep time: 10 minutes | Cook time: 25 minutes | Serves 4

- 3 baked russet potatoes, cut to 1-inch cubes
- ½ cup cooked or frozen broccoli florets
- ½ cup cooked or frozen diced onion
- 3 cloves garlic, minced
- 1 tablespoon garlic salt
- 1 tablespoon smoked paprika
- 1 teaspoon pepper
- ½ cup corn (optional)
- ½ cup cooked black beans (optional)
- ½ cup diced ham (optional)
- ½ cup crumbled cooked sausage (optional)
- ½ cup diced bacon (optional)
- cooking oil, as needed

1. Start by heating your griddle grill to medium-high heat. Pour a sufficient amount of cooking oil onto the griddle, and once it starts to glisten, arrange the diced potatoes in a single layer across the surface. Depending on their cut, potato pieces may have three or four sides; ensure each flat side cooks for 3 to 5 minutes, adding more oil as necessary. 2. While the potatoes are cooking, sauté broccoli, onion, and garlic in a separate pan for 4 to 5 minutes until they are lightly browned, stirring or flipping them occasionally to ensure even cooking. 3. When the potatoes have achieved a crispy exterior and a creamy interior, after about 10 to 12 minutes, combine the vegetable mixture with the potatoes in the griddle. Add garlic salt, smoked paprika, and pepper, and cook for an additional 2 to 3 minutes, incorporating any optional ingredients you like. Serve the dish hot for the best flavor experience.

Bacon Jalapeno–Wrapped Corn

Prep time: 10 minutes | Cook time: 20 minutes | Serves 2

- 2 ears corn, shucked
- ½ cup cream cheese, softened
- 1 tablespoon smoked paprika
- ½ cup finely diced seeded jalapeno
- 6 strips thin-cut bacon

1. Spread cream cheese over the surface of the corn to help the jalapeños stick better. Then, dust each ear of corn with paprika directly onto the cream cheese. 2. Scatter diced jalapeños on a cutting board or flat surface, and roll each ear of corn through the jalapeños, pressing down to pick up as many pieces as possible. 3. Begin wrapping each ear with a strip of bacon starting from the stalk end. Stretching the bacon slightly can create a smoother layer and help it adhere more tightly. Overlap the bacon strips as you wrap, ensuring the entire ear is covered and that the bacon is wrapped snugly to prevent the cream cheese from leaking out. 4. Preheat the griddle to a target temperature of around 300°F (150°C). 5. Place the bacon-wrapped corn directly onto the griddle, cover it, and rotate the corn a quarter turn every 2 to 3 minutes. This method aims to render the bacon fat while ensuring the corn cooks through evenly. 6. The corn should be fully cooked in about 15 to 18 minutes, with slower rendering times resulting in more flavorful bacon and corn.

Grilled Asian-Style Broccoli

Prep time: 10 minutes | Cook time: 10 minutes | Serves 4

- 4 tablespoons soy sauce
- 4 tablespoons balsamic vinegar
- 2 tablespoons canola oil
- 2 teaspoons maple syrup
- 2 heads broccoli, trimmed into florets
- Red pepper flakes, for garnish
- Sesame seeds, for garnish

1. Begin by preheating the griddle to medium-high heat. 2. As the griddle heats, whisk together soy sauce, balsamic vinegar, oil, and maple syrup in a large bowl until well combined. Add broccoli florets to the bowl and toss them until they are evenly coated with the sauce. 3. Transfer the broccoli to the grill and cook for 8 to 10 minutes, turning occasionally to ensure it is charred on all sides. 4. Once cooked, arrange the broccoli on a large serving platter, garnish with red pepper flakes and sesame seeds, and serve immediately while still warm.

Roasted Tomatoes with Hot Pepper Sauce

Prep time: 20 minutes | Cook time: 90 minutes | Serves 4 to 6

- 2 pounds (0.9 kg) roman fresh tomatoes
- 3 tablespoons parsley, chopped
- 2 tablespoons garlic, chopped
- Black pepper, to taste
- ½ cup olive oil
- Hot pepper, to taste
- 1 pound (454 g) spaghetti or other pasta

1. When you're ready to cook, set the griddle temperature to 400°F (200°C) and preheat it with the lid closed for 15 minutes. 2. Clean the tomatoes and cut them in half lengthwise, then arrange them cut-side up in a baking dish. 3. Sprinkle the tomatoes with chopped parsley and minced garlic, season with salt and black pepper, and drizzle ¼ cup of olive oil over the top. 4. Place the baking dish on the preheated griddle and bake for 1½ hours, during which time the tomatoes will reduce in size and their skins will become partially blackened. 5. Take the tomatoes out of the baking dish and transfer them to a food processor, leaving the cooked oil behind, and puree them until smooth. 6. Cook pasta in boiling salted water until al dente, then drain it and immediately toss it with the pureed tomatoes. 7. Add the remaining ¼ cup of olive oil and crumble hot red pepper over the top to taste, toss well, and serve immediately for a delicious meal. Enjoy!

Naan-Style Flatbread

Prep time: 8 minutes | Cook time: 15 minutes | Serves 8

- 1 cup warm water
- 1 teaspoon sugar
- 1 tablespoon instant dry yeast
- 3 cups all-purpose flour
- ½ cup plain yogurt
- 1 tablespoon olive oil
- 1 teaspoon salt
- cooking oil, as needed

1. In a large bowl, combine warm water, sugar, and yeast, stirring gently to mix them together. Allow the yeast to activate and bubble for approximately 10 minutes. 2. Once the yeast is active, add all the remaining ingredients except for the cooking oil, stirring until the mixture is smooth and all components are well incorporated. 3. Cover the bowl with a clean cloth and let the dough rise in a warm place for 1 hour. After it has risen, turn the dough out onto a floured surface to prepare it for cooking. 4. Preheat the griddle grill to medium heat. Divide the dough into eight equal portions, shape each into a ball, and then roll each ball out into a round that's about ¼ to ⅛ inch thick. 5. Lightly coat the griddle grill with oil and cook each dough round for 1 to 2 minutes on each side or until they have achieved a golden-brown color and a cooked texture on both sides.

Garlic and Rosemary Potato Wedges

Prep time: 15 minutes | Cook time: 1hour 30 minutes | Serves 4

- 4-6 large russet potatoes, cut into wedges
- ¼ cup olive oil
- 2 garlic cloves, minced
- 2 tablespoons rosemary leaves, chopped
- 2 teaspoons salt
- 1 teaspoon fresh ground black pepper
- 1 teaspoon sugar
- 1 teaspoon onion powder

1. Begin by preheating your griddle to 250°F. 2. In a large bowl, place the potatoes and add olive oil. 3. Toss the potatoes gently to ensure they are evenly coated with oil. 4. In a separate small bowl, combine minced garlic, salt, dried rosemary, black pepper, sugar, and onion powder. 5. Sprinkle this seasoning mix evenly over all sides of the potato wedges. 6. Transfer the seasoned potato wedges to the griddle rack and smoke cook for 1 and a half hours, or until they are tender and flavorful. 7. Finally, serve the potato wedges hot and enjoy their delicious taste!

Griddle Carrots and Asparagus

Prep time: 10 minutes | Cook time: 30 minutes | Serves 4

- 1 pound (454 g) whole carrots, with tops
- 1 bunch of asparagus, ends trimmed
- Sea salt as needed
- 1 teaspoon lemon zest
- 2 tablespoons honey
- 2 tablespoons olive oil

1. Power on the griddle or set the temperature to 450°F and allow it to preheat for at least 15 minutes. 2. In the meantime, prepare the asparagus by placing it in a medium dish, seasoning with sea salt, drizzling with oil, and tossing until evenly coated. 3. For the carrots, put them in a medium bowl, drizzle with honey, sprinkle with sea salt, and mix until they are well coated. 4. Once the griddle has reached the desired temperature, open the lid, arrange the asparagus and carrots on the griddle grate, close the griddle, and smoke cook for 30 minutes. 5. After the vegetables have finished cooking, transfer them to a serving dish, sprinkle with lemon zest for a fresh touch, and serve immediately.

Chapter 6 Vegetables and Sides

Cauliflower with Parmesan and Butter

Prep time: 15 minutes | Cook time: 45 minutes | Serves 4

- 1 medium head of cauliflower
- 1 teaspoon minced garlic
- 1 teaspoon salt
- ½ teaspoon ground black pepper
- ¼ cup olive oil
- ½ cup melted butter, unsalted
- ½ tablespoon chopped parsley
- ¼ cup shredded parmesan cheese

1. Power on the griddle, set the temperature to 450°F, and allow it to preheat for at least 15 minutes. 2. In the meantime, coat the cauliflower head with oil, season with salt and black pepper, and position it in a griddle pan. 3. Once the griddle is preheated, open the lid, place the prepared griddle pan on the griddle grate, close the griddle, and smoke cook for 45 minutes until the cauliflower is golden brown and tender in the center. 4. While the cauliflower is cooking, prepare a sauce by melting butter in a small bowl and stirring in minced garlic, chopped parsley, and grated cheese until well mixed. 5. During the last 20 minutes of cooking, baste the cauliflower with the cheese mixture regularly. After it's done, remove the pan from the heat and garnish the cauliflower with additional parsley. 6. Finally, cut the cauliflower into slices and serve hot.

Brown Sugar Glazed Smoked Acorn Squash

Prep time: 10 minutes | Cook time: 10 minutes | Serves 4

- 2 pounds (0.9 kg) acorn squash
- 3 tablespoons butter
- ¼ cup brown sugar
- ¼ teaspoon salt
- ¼ teaspoon ground cinnamon
- ¼ teaspoon ground ginger
- ¼ teaspoon ground nutmeg

1. In a bowl, combine brown sugar, salt, ground cinnamon, ground ginger, and ground nutmeg, mixing them thoroughly until well blended, and then set this spice mix aside. 2. Halve the acorn squash and place each half cut-side up in a disposable aluminum pan. 3. Spread butter over the cut surfaces of the squash and then sprinkle the prepared spice mix evenly over the top, allowing it to sit briefly. 4. Configure the griddle for indirect heat and adjust the temperature to 225°F(107 degrees Celsius). 5. Transfer the acorn squash to the griddle and smoke cook for 2 hours, or until the flesh is tender when pierced with a fork. 6. After the squash has finished cooking, remove it from the griddle and transfer it to a serving dish. 7. Serve the acorn squash warm and savor the flavors.

Vegetable Sandwich

Prep time: 10 minutes | Cook time: 10 minutes | Serves 4

For the Smoked Hummus:
- 1½ cups cooked chickpeas
- 1 tablespoon minced garlic
- 1 teaspoon salt
- 4 tablespoons lemon juice
- 2 tablespoons olive oil
- ⅓ cup tahini

For the Vegetables:
- 2 large portobello mushrooms
- 1 small eggplant, destemmed, sliced into strips
- 1 teaspoon salt
- 1 small zucchini, trimmed, sliced into strips
- ½ teaspoon ground black pepper
- 1 small yellow squash, peeled, sliced into strips
- ¼ cup olive oil

For the Cheese:
- 1 lemon, juiced
- ½ teaspoon minced garlic
- ¼ teaspoon ground black pepper
- ¼ teaspoon salt
- ½ cup ricotta cheese

To Assemble:
- 1 bunch basil, leaves chopped
- 2 heirloom tomatoes, sliced
- 4 ciabatta buns, halved

1. Activate the griddle, adjust the temperature to 180°F, and allow it to preheat for at least 15 minutes. 2. In the interim, prepare the hummus by spreading chickpeas on a sheet tray. 3. Once the griddle is preheated, open the lid, position the sheet tray on the griddle grate, close the griddle, and smoke cook for 20 minutes. 4. Afterward, transfer the chickpeas to a food processor, add the remaining hummus ingredients, and pulse for 2 minutes until smooth; set aside until needed. 5. Adjust the smoking temperature to 500°F, close the lid, and let it preheat for an additional 10 minutes. 6. While the griddle reheats, prepare the vegetables by placing them in a large bowl, seasoning with salt and black pepper, drizzling with oil and lemon juice, and tossing until evenly coated. 7. Arrange the vegetables on the griddle grate, close the lid, and smoke cook the eggplant, zucchini, and squash for 15 minutes and the mushrooms for 25 minutes. 8. Concurrently, prepare the cheese by combining its ingredients in a small bowl until well mixed. 9. Construct the sandwich by halving the buns lengthwise, spreading the prepared hummus on one side, the cheese on the other, filling with the griddle-cooked vegetables, and topping with tomatoes and basil. 10. Serve the sandwich immediately.

Chapter 6 Vegetables and Sides

Smoked Pickled Green Beans

Prep time: 15 minutes | Cook time: 45 minutes | Serves 4 to 6

- 1 pound (454 g) green beans, blanched
- ½ cup salt
- ½ cup sugar
- 1 tablespoon red pepper flake
- 2 cups white wine vinegar
- 2 cups ice water

1. When you're ready to cook, set the temperature to 180°F (82°C) and preheat the griddle with the lid closed for 15 minutes. 2. Arrange the blanched green beans on a mesh griddle mat and place this mat directly onto the griddle grate. Smoke the green beans for 30 to 45 minutes until they have absorbed the desired amount of smoke. Remove them from the griddle and set aside until the brine is prepared. 3. In a medium-sized saucepan, combine all the remaining ingredients except for the ice water, and bring them to a boil over medium-high heat on the stove. Allow the mixture to simmer for 5 to 10 minutes, then remove it from the heat and let it steep for an additional 20 minutes. Afterward, pour the brine over ice water to cool it down quickly. 4. Once the brine has cooled, pour it over the green beans and use a few plates to weigh them down, ensuring they are completely submerged. Let the green beans sit in the brine for 24 hours before using. 5. Finally, enjoy the flavorful green beans!

Smoked Tomato and Mozzarella Dip

Prep time: 5 minutes | Cook time: 1 hour | Serves 4

- 8 ounces (227 g) smoked mozzarella cheese, shredded
- 8 ounces (227 g) Copoundy cheese, shredded
- ½ cup parmesan cheese, grated
- 1 cup sour cream
- 1 cup sun-dried tomatoes
- 1½ teaspoons salt
- 1 teaspoon fresh ground pepper
- 1 teaspoon dried basil
- 1 teaspoon dried oregano
- 1 teaspoon red pepper flakes
- 1 garlic clove, minced
- ½ teaspoon onion powder
- French toast, serving

1. Begin by preheating your griddle to 275°F. 2. In a large bowl, combine cheeses, diced tomatoes, pepper, salt, fresh basil, oregano, red pepper flakes, minced garlic, and onion powder, mixing thoroughly until all ingredients are well incorporated. 3. Pour this mixture into a small metal baking pan and then place the pan onto the griddle. 4. Allow the mixture to smoke cook for 1 hour. 5. Once cooked, serve the cheesy mixture with toasted French bread on the side. 6. Enjoy your delicious creation!

Griddle Fingerling Potato Salad

Prep time: 15 minutes | Cook time: 15 minutes | Serves 6-8

- 1½ pounds (680 g) Fingerling potatoes cut in half lengthwise
- 10 scallions
- ⅔ cup Evo (extra virgin olive oil), divided use
- 2 tablespoons rice vinegar
- 2 teaspoons lemon juice
- 1 small jalapeno, sliced
- 2 teaspoons kosher salt

1. When you're ready to cook, set the griddle to High heat, close the lid, and preheat for 15 minutes. Brush the scallions with oil and place them on the griddle to cook until they are lightly charred, which should take about 2 to 3 minutes. Remove the scallions from the griddle and allow them to cool. Once cooled, slice them thinly and set aside. 2. Brush the Fingerling potatoes with oil (saving ⅓ cup for later), then season with salt and pepper. Place them cut-side down on the griddle and cook until they are tender throughout, which should take around 4 to 5 minutes. 3. In a bowl, whisk together the remaining ⅓ cup of olive oil, rice vinegar, salt, and lemon juice to create a dressing. Mix in the cooled scallions, cooked potatoes, and sliced jalapeño, and season with additional salt and pepper to taste. Serve immediately and enjoy the flavorful dish!

Healthy Zucchini Noodles

Prep time: 10 minutes | Cook time: 10 minutes | Serves 4

- 4 small zucchini, spiralized
- 1 tablespoon soy sauce
- 2 onions, spiralized
- 2 tablespoons olive oil
- 1 tablespoon sesame seeds
- 2 tablespoons teriyaki sauce

1. Start by preheating the griddle to high heat. 2. Once the griddle is hot, add oil to the surface. 3. Toss in the onions and sauté them for about 4 to 5 minutes until they become translucent and slightly golden. 4. Add zucchini noodles to the pan and cook for an additional 2 minutes. 5. Stir in sesame seeds, teriyaki sauce, and soy sauce, and continue cooking for another 4 to 5 minutes until the flavors meld together. Serve hot and enjoy the delicious meal.

Beer Smoked Cabbage with Garlic Rub

Prep time: 40 minutes | Cook time: 3 hours | Serves 10

- 3 pounds (1.36 kg) whole cabbages
- 3 tablespoons olive oil
- 2 teaspoons garlic powder
- ¼ teaspoon salt
- ¼ teaspoon chili powder
- ½ teaspoon ground cinnamon
- 1 can beer

1. In a bowl, combine garlic powder, salt, chili powder, and ground cinnamon. 2. Drizzle olive oil over the spices and mix them thoroughly until they form a cohesive blend. 3. Rub the spice mixture evenly over the cabbage, making sure to distribute it between the leaves as well. 4. Configure the griddle for indirect heat and adjust the temperature to 275°F (135°C). 5. Place the seasoned cabbage on a sheet of aluminum foil, wrap it up with the top left open for ventilation. 6. Pour beer over the wrapped cabbage and place it on the griddle to smoke cook for 3 hours, or until the cabbage is tender when pierced with a fork. 7. After the cabbage has finished cooking, remove it from the griddle and unwrap it carefully. 8. Cut the smoked cabbage into wedges and serve immediately. 9. Enjoy your delicious smoked cabbage!

Griddle-Grilled Veggie Egg Rolls

Prep time: 10 minutes | Cook time: 20 minutes | Serves 8

- 8 egg roll wrappers
- 4 cups bagged coleslaw mix (shredded cabbage and carrots)
- 2 tablespoons ginger paste
- 2 tablespoons soy sauce
- 2 tablespoons sesame oil
- 1 tablespoon garlic powder
- 1 teaspoon ground ginger
- cooking oil, as needed

1. Keep the egg roll wrappers sealed until you are ready to assemble the egg rolls. In a large bowl, mix all the ingredients except for the cooking oil, ensuring that the vegetables are well coated with the spices. 2. Preheat the griddle grill to medium heat. Cook the vegetable mixture until the cabbage wilts, the carrots soften, and the mixture releases moisture, which should reduce its size by roughly a third. Transfer the cooked mixture to a few paper towels to absorb any excess moisture and let it cool to at least room temperature. 3. Egg roll wrappers are like raw pasta sheets and can dry out quickly if exposed to air for extended periods. To prevent this, cover the wrappers you're not using and keep them away from liquids. To assemble an egg roll, place a wrapper on a dry surface, spoon about ¼ cup of the vegetable mixture onto the bottom third, leaving a border about the width of your pointer finger from the edges. Dip your fingers in a small bowl of water and moisten the edges of the wrapper, then fold the sides over the filling and pinch them in place. Roll the wrapper tightly over the filling, ensuring the filling stays inside and the sides are sealed. Place the egg roll seam-side down on a dry tray and repeat with the remaining ingredients. 4. Increase the griddle grill to medium-high heat, add the cooking oil, and once it shimmers, place the egg rolls seam-side down on the griddle. Cook without moving them for 3 to 4 minutes to seal the egg rolls. Carefully roll the egg rolls to brown the other sides of the wrappers, adding more oil if needed. Since the vegetables are already cooked, this step is to brown the wrappers and reheat the vegetables.

Chapter 7
Snacks and Appetizers

Chapter 7 Snacks and Appetizers

Golden Sweet Potato Fries

Prep time: 10 minutes | Cook time: 12 minutes | Serves 4

- 2 pounds (0.9 kg) peeled and cut into ½-inch wedges sweet potatoes
- 2 tablespoons olive oil
- pepper and salt to taste

Intolerances:
- Gluten-Free Egg-Free
- Lactose-Free

1. Preheat the griddle to medium-high heat. 2. Toss sweet potatoes with oil, pepper, and salt. 3. Place sweet potato wedges on a hot griddle and cook over a medium heat for 6 minutes. 4. Flip and cook for 6-8 minutes more. Serve.

Ramen Noodle Pork and Veggie Patty

Prep time: 10 minutes | Cook time: 15 minutes | Serves 2

- ¼ pound (113g) ground pork
- ¼ cup soy sauce
- 2 tablespoons minced ginger
- 2 tablespoons minced garlic
- 2 tablespoons sesame oil
- 2 (6-ounce / 170g) packages cooked ramen noodles
- 2 cups chopped cabbage
- ¾ cup chopped kale
- ⅓ cup shredded carrot
- Asian Griddle Sauce, as needed
- cooking oil, as needed

1. Bring the griddle grill to medium-high heat. Place the ground pork on the griddle and using a spatula, or spatula and scraper, cook the pork, chopping it into fine pieces to promote even cooking and texture. 2. After about 4 minutes, add the soy sauce, ginger, garlic, and sesame oil to the pork. Continue to cook for another 1 to 2 minutes until the liquids have reduced, and slide to a cooler area on the griddle. 3. Add oil to your cooking surface and allow it to heat until shimmering. Spread the cooked ramen noodles in a thin layer across the griddle, taking advantage of the surface area it provides. The noodles are hydrated with water, and we want the water to evaporate some, eventually making the noodles crispy. In the process, the noodles will go from wet to gooey and gummy, and then begin turning brown and crispy. It is important to allow the noodles to cook, but not burn on the griddle. When you first flip the noodles, after about 5 minutes, work in batches and make sure to scrape as many of the noodle bits from the grilling surface as you can. Add more oil as needed to prevent sticking and promote browning, but use it sparingly. 4. Add the cabbage, kale, carrot, and pork onto half of the noodles. Layer the other noodles on top of the mixture and allow the noodles to help wilt the veggies. Spread all the ingredients out across the griddle and flip the noodles and veggies from the outside inward to help the veggies make more contact with the griddle, and add some Asian Griddle Sauce for additional flavor. 5. As the griddle sauce reduces, and eventually evaporates, you will notice the noodles and veggies start to brown and get quite crispy. This is what you are after. The outer layer of the noodle cake should be crispy and crunchy, and the inner noodles should still be a bit supple, balancing the textures.

Classic Buttered Popcorn

Prep time: 8 minutes | Cook time: 8 minutes | Serves 3

- 3 tablespoons peanut oil
- ½ cup popcorn kernels
- 3 tablespoons butter
- salt, to taste

1. Prepare your griddle for two-zone cooking. 2. Bring the griddle grill to medium-high heat and add the peanut oil. While it is heating, place 5 popcorn kernels in the oil. When 2 or 3 pop, add the butter to the oil and pour in the remaining kernels. Cover immediately with a tall pan or spaghetti pot. 3. When the popcorn starts popping, you will need to stir it in the oil to get all the kernels to pop and prevent the popped corn from burning. Using insulated gloves, potholders, or thick kitchen towels, agitate the popcorn by moving the pan or pot from side to side on the griddle without lifting. Cook for about 4 minutes, or until the popping slows down to once every few seconds. 4. When all the corn is popped, slide the pot or pan and popcorn to the cool side of the grill and remove the lid. Use two spatulas to scoop up the hot popcorn and transfer to a bowl. Serve with salt and additional seasonings as desired.

Crunchy Spiced Chickpeas

Prep time: 10 minutes | Cook time: 30 minutes | Serves 2

- 1 (16 ounces / 454 g) can chickpeas, drained
- ¼ cup olive oil
- 1 tablespoon ground cumin
- 1 tablespoon smoked paprika
- 1 teaspoon garlic powder
- 1 teaspoon onion powder
- 1 teaspoon kosher salt, plus more to taste

1. Combine all ingredients in a large bowl. 2. Pour the mixture onto a cool griddle grill and bring the griddle to medium heat. 3. Allow the mixture to slowly come to temperature and continue to cook, stirring frequently, for up to 30 minutes or until the garbanzo beans have lost most of their moisture and become crispy and crunchy. Finish with additional salt, if desired.

Quesadilla Bun Chicken Fajita Melt

Prep time: 15 minutes | Cook time: 25 minutes | Serves 2

For the fajita chicken marinade:
- ½ cup cooking oil
- 1 ounce (28g) tequila
- 2 tablespoons Worcestershire sauce
- 1 tablespoon hot sauce
- 4 cloves garlic, minced
- juice of 1 lemon
- juice of 1 lime
- 1 tablespoon ground cumin
- 1 tablespoon garlic powder
- 1 tablespoon onion powder
- 1 teaspoon salt
- 1 teaspoon pepper

For the fajitas:
- 1 (8-ounce / 227g) chicken breast, sliced into strips
- ½ Lemon Griddle Sauce, plus more for cooking
- 8 medium-sized flour tortillas
- 2 cups shredded cheddar-Jack cheese blend
- ½ green bell pepper, cut into strips
- ½ red bell pepper, cut into strips
- 1 medium, sweet onion cut into strips
- ¾ cup prepared salsa, divided
- salt and pepper, to taste

1. Mix all the fajita marinade ingredients together in a large bowl. Add the sliced chicken to the mixture, cover, and allow to marinate in refrigerator for 4 to 6 hours or overnight. 2. Bring the griddle grill to medium-high heat. Place the chicken on the grill. Discard any leftover marinade. Cook the chicken strips, covered, for 10 to 12 minutes until cooked through, turning occasionally and adding Lemon Griddle Sauce from time to time to promote steaming. 3. While the chicken is cooking, place four of the tortillas on the griddle and allow them to warm. As the tortillas begin to warm, divide the cheese between them and cover each with a second tortilla to make the quesadilla buns. Flip the quesadillas after 3 minutes and allow the other sides to warm and the cheese to melt for another 3 minutes. Set aside and keep warm. 4. Warm a little oil on the grill, add the peppers and onions, and allow to sauté for 3 to 5 minutes until wilted. As peppers and onions begin to wilt, sprinkle with salt and pepper, add about ½ cup Lemon Griddle Sauce, and cook for about 3 more minutes, until the onions are translucent. 5. When the chicken is fully cooked, assemble by placing a quesadilla on a plate and covering with salsa. Add chicken, peppers and onions, and top with an additional quesadilla.

Savory Crab-Filled Mushrooms

Prep time: 20 minutes | Cook time: 30 to 45 minutes | Serves 6

- 6 medium-sized portobello mushrooms
- extra virgin olive oil

club beat staffing:
- 8 ounces (227 g) fresh crab meat or canned or imitation crab meat
- 2 tablespoons extra virgin olive oil
- ⅓ chopped celery
- chopped red peppers
- ½ cup chopped green onion
- ½ cup italian breadcrumbs
- ½ cup mayonnaise
- ⅓ grated parmesan cheese cup
- 8 ounces (227 g) cream cheese at room temperature
- ½ teaspoon of garlic
- 1 tablespoon dried parsley
- grated parmesan cheese cup
- 1 teaspoon of old bay seasoning
- ¼ teaspoon of kosher salt
- ¼ teaspoon black pepper

Intolerances:
- egg-free

1. Clean the mushroom cap with a damp paper towel. Cut off the stem and save it. 2. Remove the brown gills from the bottom of the mushroom cap with a spoon and discard. 3. Prepare crab meat stuffing. If you are using canned crab meat, drain, rinse, and remove shellfish. 4. Heat the olive oil in a frying pan over medium high heat. Add celery, peppers and green onions and fry for 5 minutes. Set aside for cooling. 5. Gently pour the chilled sautéed vegetables and the remaining ingredients into a large bowl. 6. Cover and refrigerate crab meat stuffing until ready to use. 7. Put the crab mixture in each mushroom cap and make a mound in the center. 8. Sprinkle extra virgin olive oil and sprinkle parmesan cheese on each stuffed mushroom cap. Put the mushrooms in a 10 x 15-inch baking dish. 9. Use the griddle to indirect heating and preheat to 375°F. 10. Bake for 30-45 minutes until the filling becomes hot (165°F (74°C) as measured by an instant-read digital thermometer) and the mushrooms begin to release juice.

Cheddar Bacon Sliders

Prep time: 30 minutes | Cook time: 15 minutes | Serves 2

- 1 pound (454 g) ground beef (80% lean)
- ½ teaspoon of garlic salt
- ½ teaspoon salt
- ½ teaspoon of garlic
- ½ teaspoon onion
- ½ teaspoon black pepper
- 6 bacon slices, cut in half
- ½ cup mayonnaise
- 2 teaspoons of creamy wasabi (optional)
- 6 (1 ounce / 27 g) sliced sharp cheddar cheese, cut in half (optional)
- Sliced red onion
- ½ cup sliced kosher dill pickles
- 12 mini breads sliced horizontally
- Ketchup

Intolerances:

- Egg-Free

1. Place ground beef, garlic salt, seasoned salt, garlic powder, onion powder and black pepper in a medium bowl. 2. Divide the meat mixture into 12 equal parts, shape into small thin round patties (about 2 ounces (57 g) each) and save. 3. Cook the bacon on medium heat over medium heat for 5-8 minutes until crunchy. Set aside. 4. To make the sauce, mix the mayonnaise and horseradish in a small bowl, if used. 5. Preheat griddle to 350°F. Griddle surface should be approximately 400°F. 6. Spray a cooking spray on the griddle cooking surface for best non-stick results. 7. Griddle the putty for 3-4 minutes each until the internal temperature reaches 160°F. 8. If necessary, place a sharp cheddar cheese slice on each patty while the patty is on the griddle or after the patty is removed from the griddle. 9. Place a small amount of mayonnaise mixture, a slice of red onion, and a hamburger pate in the lower half of each roll. 10. Pickled slices, bacon and ketchup.

Herb-Seasoned Potato Sticks

Prep time: 15 minutes | Cook time: 25 minutes | Serves 8

- 2 pounds (0.9 kg) quartered potatoes
- 1 teaspoon garlic powder
- 2 teaspoons crushed dried rosemary
- 4 tablespoons dry white wine
- ½ cup mayonnaise
- ½ cup water

Intolerances:

- Gluten-Free
- Egg-Free
- Lactose-Free

1. Add potatoes and water in a microwave-safe bowl and cook in the microwave for 15 minutes or until potatoes are tender. 2. Drain potatoes well and let them cool. In a large mixing bowl, stir together mayonnaise, garlic powder, rosemary, and wine. 3. Add potatoes and toss to coat. Cover bowl and place in the refrigerator for 1 hour. 4. Preheat the griddle to a high heat and oil grates. Remove potatoes from the marinade and thread onto the skewers. 5. Place potato skewers on a hot griddle, cover, and cook for 6-8 minutes. Turn skewers halfway through. 6. Serve.

Glazed Balsamic Mushroom Skewers

Prep time: 10 minutes | Cook time: 10 minutes | Serves 4

- 2 pounds (0.9 kg) sliced ¼-inch thick mushrooms
- ½ teaspoon chopped thyme
- 3 chopped garlic cloves

Intolerances:
- Gluten-Free
- Egg-Free

- 1 tablespoon soy sauce
- 2 tablespoons balsamic vinegar
- pepper and salt to taste

- Lactose-Free

1. Add mushrooms and remaining ingredients into the mixing bowl, cover, and place in the refrigerator for 30 minutes. 2. Thread marinated mushrooms onto the skewers. 3. Heat the griddle to medium-high heat. Place mushroom skewers onto the hot griddle and cook for 2-3 minutes per side. 4. Serve.

Tomatoes with Parmesan Cheese

Prep time: 2 hours | Cook time: 20 minutes | Serves 6

- 9 halved Tomatoes
- 1 cup grated Parmesan cheese
- ½ teaspoon Ground black pepper
- ¼ teaspoon Onion powder

Intolerances:
- Gluten-Free

- 1 tablespoon Dried rosemary
- 2 tablespoons Olive oil
- 5 minced Garlic cloves
- 1 teaspoon Kosher salt

- Egg-Free

1. Heat a griddle to medium-low heat and oil grates. 2. Place tomatoes halves cut side down, onto the griddle and cook for 5-7 minutes. 3. Heat olive oil in a pan over a medium heat. Add garlic, rosemary, black pepper, onion powder, and salt and cook for 3-5 minutes. 4. Remove from heat and set aside. Flip each tomato half and brush with olive oil garlic mixture and top with grated parmesan cheese. 5. Close griddle and cook for 7-10 minutes more until cheese is melted. 6. Remove tomatoes from the griddle and serve immediately.

Chapter 8

Desserts

Chapter 8 Desserts

Bacon Chocolate Chip Cookies

Prep time: 30 minutes | Cook time: 30 minutes | Serves 6

- 8 slices cooked and crumbled bacon
- 2½ teaspoons apple cider vinegar
- 1 teaspoon vanilla
- 2 cups semisweet chocolate chips
- 2 room temp eggs
- 1½ teaspoons baking soda
- 1 cup granulated sugar
- ½ teaspoon salt
- 2¾ cups all-purpose flour
- 1 cup light brown sugar
- 1½ stick softened butter

1. In a bowl, mix together salt, baking soda, and flour. 2. In a separate bowl, cream sugar and butter until light and fluffy, then reduce the mixer speed. Gradually add eggs, vinegar, and vanilla extract, mixing well after each addition. 3. Turn the heat to low on your stove, and slowly incorporate the flour mixture into the wet ingredients, followed by bacon pieces and chocolate chips, stirring continuously. 4. Preheat your griddle with the lid closed until it reaches 375°F. 5. Line a baking sheet with parchment paper and drop rounded teaspoonfuls of cookie batter onto it. Place the baking sheet on the griddle, cover, and cook for approximately 12 minutes or until the cookies are golden brown around the edges.

S'mores Dip

Prep time: 10 minutes | Cook time: 25 minutes | Serves 8

- 12 ounces (340 g) semisweet chocolate chips
- ¼ cup milk
- 2 tablespoons melted salted butter
- 16 ounces (453 g) marshmallows
- Apple wedges
- Graham crackers

1. Preheat your griddle with the lid closed until it reaches 450°F. 2. Place a cast iron griddle pan on top of your griddle, pour in the milk and melted butter, and stir them together for about a minute to combine. 3. Once the mixture has heated up, sprinkle the chocolate chips on top to form a single layer, then position the marshmallows vertically on top of the chocolate, ensuring they cover as much of the chocolate as possible. 4. Cover the griddle and let it smoke cook for five to seven minutes, or until the marshmallows are lightly toasted. 5. Finally, remove the griddle from the heat and serve the s'mores with apple wedges and graham crackers for an enjoyable treat!

Blackberry Pie

Prep time: 15 minutes | Cook time: 40 minutes | Serves 8

- Butter, for greasing
- ½ cup all-purpose flour
- ½ cup milk
- 2 pints blackberries
- 2 cup sugar, divided
- 1 box refrigerated piecrusts
- 1 stick melted butter
- 1 stick of butter
- Vanilla ice cream

1. Preheat your griddle with the lid closed until it reaches 375°F. 2. Butter a cast iron griddle pan. 3. Unroll a pie crust and transfer it to the griddle, pressing it into the bottom and up the sides. Use a fork to poke holes in the crust for ventilation. 4. Place the griddle with the crust on the griddle and smoke cook for five minutes, or until the crust is golden brown. Remove it from the griddle. 5. In a bowl, mix together 1½ cups of sugar, flour, and melted butter, then add blackberries and toss to combine. 6. Pour the berry mixture into the crust, followed by the milk, and sprinkle half of the diced butter on top. 7. Unroll the second pie crust and lay it over the filling. Alternatively, slice it into strips and weave it on top to create a lattice design. Place the remaining diced butter over the top. 8. Sprinkle the rest of the sugar over the crust, then place the griddle with the pie back on the griddle. Lower the lid and smoke cook for 15 to 20 minutes, or until the crust is browned and the filling is bubbly. Consider covering the pie with foil during the last few minutes to prevent burning. Serve the hot pie with a scoop of vanilla ice cream for a delicious dessert.

Griddle Layered Cake

Prep time: 10 minutes | Cook time: 20 minutes | Serves 6

- 2 pounds (0.9 kg) cake
- 3 cups of whipped cream
- ¼ cup melted butter
- 1 cup of blueberries
- 1 cup of raspberries
- 1 cup sliced strawberries

1. Preheat the griddle to high heat with the lid closed. 2. Slice the cake loaf into ¾-inch-thick pieces, aiming for about 10 slices per loaf. Brush both sides of each slice with butter. 3. Place the cake slices on the griddle and cook for 7 minutes on each side. Remove them from the griddle and set aside to cool. 4. Once the cake slices have cooled completely, begin layering your cake by placing a slice of cake on a serving plate, followed by a layer of berries and a dollop of cream. Repeat this process until you've used all your cake slices. 5. Finally, sprinkle the top of the cake with additional berries and serve as a delicious dessert.

White Chocolate Bread Pudding

Prep time: 20 minutes | Cook time: 1hour | Serves 12

- 1 loaf french bread
- 4 cups heavy cream
- 3 large eggs
- 2 cups white sugar
- 1 package white chocolate morsels
- ¼ cup melted butter
- 2 teaspoons vanilla
- 1 teaspoon ground nutmeg
- 1 teaspoon salt
- bourbon white chocolate sauce
- 1 package white chocolate morsels
- 1 cup heavy cream
- 2 tablespoons melted butter
- 2 tablespoons bourbon
- ½ teaspoon salt

1. Preheat the griddle to 350°F. 2. Tear French bread into small pieces and place them in a large bowl. Pour four cups of heavy cream over the bread and let it soak for 30 minutes. 3. In a medium bowl, combine eggs, sugar, softened butter, and vanilla extract. Add a package of white chocolate chips and a delicate blend of spices, then season with nutmeg and salt. 4. Pour the egg mixture over the soaked bread and mix well to combine. 5. Pour the mixture into a well-buttered 9x13-inch baking dish and place it on the griddle. 6. Cook for 60 seconds or until the bread pudding has set and the top has darkened slightly. 7. For the sauce, melt margarine in a saucepan over medium heat. Add whiskey and continue cooking for three to four minutes until the alcohol has evaporated and the margarine begins to darken. 8. Stir in heavy cream and heat until the sauce is warmed through. Remove from heat and gradually add white chocolate chips, stirring continuously until all are melted and the sauce is smooth. Season with a hint of salt and serve over the bread pudding.

Apple Cobbler

Prep time: 30 minutes | Cook time: 1 hour 50 minutes | Serves 8

- 8 Granny Smith apples
- 1 cup sugar
- 1 stick melted butter
- 1 teaspoon cinnamon
- Pinch salt
- ½ cup brown sugar
- 2 eggs
- 2 teaspoons baking powder
- 2 cups plain flour
- 1½ cups sugar

1. Peel and quarter apples, then place them into a bowl. Add cinnamon and one cup of sugar, stir well to coat the apples, and let the mixture sit for one hour. 2. Preheat your griddle with the lid closed until it reaches 350°F. 3. In a large bowl, combine salt, baking powder, eggs, brown sugar, granulated sugar, and flour, mixing until the ingredients form crumbles. 4. Arrange the apples in a baking dish or griddle pan, sprinkle the crumble mixture evenly over the top, and drizzle with melted butter. 5. Place the dish on the preheated griddle and cook for 50 minutes, or until the crumble topping is golden brown and the apples are tender.

Grilled Pineapple With Maple Walnut Ice Cream

Prep time: 5 minutes | Cook time: 5 minutes | Serves 8

- 1 pineapple, cored and cut into rings, or 1 (16 ounces / 454 g) can pineapple rings
- ¼ cup maple syrup
- juice of 1 lime
- ¼ teaspoon ground cinnamon
- butter, clarified butter, or coconut oil
- 1 pint maple walnut ice cream, to serve
- chocolate sauce, to serve

1. Preheat the griddle grill to medium heat. In a small bowl, combine maple syrup, lime juice, and cinnamon, and set this syrup mixture aside. 2. Apply a thin layer of butter or oil to the griddle grill. Place the pineapple rings in the oil and cook for 3 to 4 minutes, flipping them frequently to ensure even cooking. Keep a close eye and use your sense of smell; if you detect burning, promptly move the pineapple to a cooler section of the griddle. 3. Once the pineapple rings have achieved a golden hue, brush both sides with the maple-lime syrup. Cook for an additional 45 seconds on each side before removing them from the griddle. 4. Serve the pineapple rings with a small scoop of maple walnut ice cream and a drizzle of chocolate sauce for a delicious dessert.

Cinnamon Sugar Pumpkin Seeds

Prep time: 15 minutes | Cook time: 30 minutes | Serves 8

- 2 tablespoons sugar
- Seeds from a pumpkin
- 1 teaspoon cinnamon
- 2 tablespoons melted butter

1. Preheat your griddle with the lid closed until it reaches 350°F. 2. Clean the seeds and toss them in melted butter, then add them to a mixture of sugar and cinnamon. Spread the seasoned seeds out on a baking sheet, place the sheet on the griddle, and smoke cook for 25 minutes. 3. Serve the seeds warm as a snack or topping for desserts.

Juicy Loosey Cheeseburger

Prep time: 10 minutes | Cook time: 10 minutes | Serves 6

- 2 pounds (0.9 kg) ground beef
- 1 egg beaten
- 1 cup dry bread crumbs
- 3 tablespoons evaporated milk
- 2 tablespoons worcestershire sauce
- 1 tablespoons griddlea griddles all purpose rub
- 4 slices of cheddar cheese
- 4 buns

1. Begin by combining the hamburger meat, egg, evaporated milk, Worcestershire sauce, and focus into a bowl. Use your hands to mix well, then divide this mixture into four equal parts. Further divide each part into smaller equal portions and shape them into smooth patties. The goal is to create eight evenly sized flat patties that you will then combine into four burgers. 2. Once you have your patties shaped, place a slice of cheese in the center of one patty, then place another patty on top and firmly press the sides to seal. You may need to push some meat back towards the center to create a slightly thicker patty. The patties should be slightly larger than a standard burger bun as they will shrink a bit during cooking. 3. Preheat your griddle or grill to 300°F. 4. Remember that during grilling, you essentially have two thin patties, one on each side, so the cooking time should be adjusted accordingly. Cook these for 5 to 8 minutes per side—closer to 5 minutes if you prefer a rare burger or closer to 8 minutes if you like your burger well-done. 5. When you flip the burgers, insert a toothpick into the center to allow steam to escape. This will prevent the burger from bursting open or a guest from getting a burnt mouthful from melted cheese as they take their first bite. 6. Place these burgers on a nice roll and top with fixings that complement whatever toppings your burgers have.

Chocolate Chip Cookies

Prep time: 30 minutes | Cook time: 30 minutes | Serves 8

- 1½ cups chopped walnuts
- 1 teaspoon vanilla
- 2 cups chocolate chips
- 1 teaspoon baking soda
- 2½ cups plain flour
- ½ teaspoon salt
- 1½ stick softened butter
- 2 eggs
- 1 cup brown sugar
- ½ cup sugar

1. Preheat your griddle with the lid closed until it reaches 350°F. 2. In a small bowl, mix together baking soda, salt, and flour. 3. In a larger bowl, cream together brown sugar, granulated sugar, and butter until light and fluffy. Mix in vanilla and eggs until the mixture comes together smoothly. 4. Gradually add the flour mixture to the wet ingredients while continuing to beat. Once all the flour is incorporated, add chocolate chips and walnuts, then fold the batter gently with a spoon. 5. Place a sheet of aluminum foil on the griddle, drop rounded spoonfuls of dough onto it, and bake for 17 minutes or until the cookies are golden brown around the edges.

Appendix 1: Measurement Conversion Chart

VOLUME EQUIVALENTS(DRY)

US STANDARD	METRIC (APPROXIMATE)
1/8 teaspoon	0.5 mL
1/4 teaspoon	1 mL
1/2 teaspoon	2 mL
3/4 teaspoon	4 mL
1 teaspoon	5 mL
1 tablespoon	15 mL
1/4 cup	59 mL
1/2 cup	118 mL
3/4 cup	177 mL
1 cup	235 mL
2 cups	475 mL
3 cups	700 mL
4 cups	1 L

WEIGHT EQUIVALENTS

US STANDARD	METRIC (APPROXIMATE)
1 ounce	28 g
2 ounces	57 g
5 ounces	142 g
10 ounces	284 g
15 ounces	425 g
16 ounces (1 pound)	455 g
1.5 pounds	680 g
2 pounds	907 g

VOLUME EQUIVALENTS(LIQUID)

US STANDARD	US STANDARD (OUNCES)	METRIC (APPROXIMATE)
2 tablespoons	1 fl.oz.	30 mL
1/4 cup	2 fl.oz.	60 mL
1/2 cup	4 fl.oz.	120 mL
1 cup	8 fl.oz.	240 mL
1 1/2 cup	12 fl.oz.	355 mL
2 cups or 1 pint	16 fl.oz.	475 mL
4 cups or 1 quart	32 fl.oz.	1 L
1 gallon	128 fl.oz.	4 L

TEMPERATURES EQUIVALENTS

FAHRENHEIT(F)	CELSIUS(C) (APPROXIMATE)
225 °F	107 °C
250 °F	120 °C
275 °F	135 °C
300 °F	150 °C
325 °F	160 °C
350 °F	180 °C
375 °F	190 °C
400 °F	205 °C
425 °F	220 °C
450 °F	235 °C
475 °F	245 °C
500 °F	260 °C

Appendix 2: Recipes Index

A

Apple Cobbler	65
Artisanal Grilled Pizza with Eggs and Greens	5
Asian-Spiced Seared Salmon	25

B

Bacon Chocolate Chip Cookies	64
Bacon Jalapeno Wraps	44
Bacon Jalapeno–Wrapped Corn	53
Basil Pesto Grilled Shrimp	26
Basil-Ginger Shrimp Burgers	48
BBQ Hen	18
BBQ Pulled Turkey Sandwiches	21
Beer Smoked Cabbage with Garlic Rub	57
Bell Peppers Stuffed with Eggs and Crispy Bacon	40
Big Burger	46
Blackberry Pie	64
Blistered Green Beans	52
Bone-In Chicken Thighs with Caramelized Fish Sauce	18
Brown Sugar Glazed Smoked Acorn Squash	55
Buffalo Chicken Thighs	13

C

Caesar Marinated Griddle Chicken	16
Cajun-Style Seared Salmon	26
Cauliflower with Parmesan and Butter	55
Cheddar Bacon Sliders	61
Cheese and Beef Patty Melt	37
Chicken and Vegetable Kebabs	15
Chicken Breasts Griddle With Feta And Fresh Mint	13
Chicken Fajitas	20
Chicken Fried Rice	13
Chicken Roast with Pineapple Salsa	14
Chicken Satay With Thai Peanut Sauce	15
Chicken Thighs With Ginger-Sesame Glaze	14
Chile-Lime Clams with Tomato and Flatbread	29
Chipotle Adobe Chicken	17
Chipotle Burgers With Avocado	47
Chocolate Chip Cookies	66
Cinnamon Sugar Pumpkin Seeds	66
Classic BBQ Chicken	19
Classic Buttered Popcorn	59
Classic Roast Beef Sandwich	38
Cod Fillets in Savory Onion Butter	28
Cool and Creamy Ice Cream French Toast	9
Corn & Cheese Chile Rellenos	52
Creamy Buttermilk Pancakes	4
Crispy Fried Pickles	8
Crispy Hash Brown Scramble	4
Crispy Potato Pancakes	8
Crunchy Spiced Chickpeas	60
Crusted Blackened Tilapia	27
Cured Turkey Drumstick	16

D

Decadent Bacon Egg and Cheese Sandwich	10
Delightful Toad in a Hole	7
Dijon and Paprika-Spiced Pork Tenderloin	33
Diner-Style Omelet	6

E

Elegant Denver Omelet	11
Elegant Eggs Belledict	9
Espresso-Crusted Skirt Steak	37

F

Fiery Cajun Pork Cutlets	37
Fiery Grilled Squid	30
Filet Mignon with Caprese Topping	38
Flaky and Light Crepes	8
Flank Steak Gyros with Greek Herbs	35
Flavorful Chorizo Breakfast Tacos	5
Flavorful Cornish Game Hen	16

G

Garlic and Rosemary Potato Wedges	54
Garlicky Pork Burgers	47
Glazed Balsamic Mushroom Skewers	62
Golden Johnny Cakes	4
Golden Sweet Potato Fries	59
Griddle Carrots and Asparagus	54
Griddle Fingerling Potato Salad	56
Griddle Layered Cake	65

Griddle Pizza Cheese	47
Griddle Sugar Snap Peas	51
Griddle Vegetable Pizza	45
Griddle-Grilled Veggie Egg Rolls	57
Grilled Asian-Style Broccoli	53
Grilled Coconut-Pineapple Shrimp Skewers	24
Grilled Cuttlefish and Spinach Pine Nut Medley	23
Grilled Fish with Fresh Salsa Verde	26
Grilled Halibut Fillets in Spicy Rosemary Marinade	25
Grilled Lobster Tails with Lime-Basil Butter	27
Grilled Pineapple With Maple Walnut Ice Cream	65
Grilled Prawn Skewers with Fresh Parsley	25
Grilled Salmon Fillet Skewers	30
Grilled Salmon Steaks with Herbed Yogurt-Cilantro Drizzle	24
Grilled Shrimp in Spicy Lemon Butter	24
Grilled Shrimp with Polenta Cheese Cakes	29
Grilled Vegetable Pizza	48

H

Habanero-Infused Grilled Pork Chops	34
Hasselback Stuffed Chicken	17
Healthy Zucchini Noodles	56
Hearty Potato Bacon Hash	7
Hearty Sausage and Vegetable Scramble	10
Hearty Ultimate Breakfast Burrito	7
Herb-Seasoned Potato Sticks	61
Hoisin Turkey Wings	15
Home Fries With Veggies	53
Honey Balsamic Marinated Chicken	14
Honey-Soy Glazed Pork Chop	34
Hot Sauce Smoked Turkey Tabasco	20

J

Jalapeno Injection Turkey	19
Juicy Loosey Cheeseburger	66

K

Kale Caesar Salad With Seared Chicken	21

L

Lemon-Garlic Artichokes	51
Light and Fluffy Blueberry Pancakes	11
Loaded Bacon Monster Burgers	42
Lobster Tails with a Hint of Lemon	31

M

Marinated Beef Skewers	34
Marinated Carne Asada Strips	37
Mediterranean-Style Salmon	28
Mini Portobello Burgers	46

N

Naan-Style Flatbread	54
New Mexican Salsa Verde	47
New York-Style Chopped Beef and Cheese	40

O

Open-Faced Clams with Spicy Horseradish Sauce	27
Orange Cornish Hen	17

P

Paprika-Garlic Seared Shrimp	30
Perfectly Cooked NY Strip Steak	36
Pineapple Teriyaki Turkey Burgers	45
Pineapple-Glazed Beef Burger	40
Pork Chops Topped with Herbed Apple Relish	40
Pork Shoulder in Peach Mojo Sauce	38
Pork Tenderloin with a Mediterranean Herb Crust	36

Q

Quesadilla Bun Chicken Fajita Melt	60

R

Radiant Golden Hash Browns	11
Radish Browns With Black Beans And Red Peppers	52
Ramen Noodle Pork and Veggie Patty	59
Ribeye Pork Loin Florentine Style	41
Roast Beef and Tomato Sandwich	42
Roasted Tomatoes with Hot Pepper Sauce	54
Rosemary Butter Cornish Hens	15
Rustic Tuscan Steak and Golden Potatoes	41

S

S'mores Dip	64
Sage Thyme Cornish Hen	18
Salmon Burgers	49
Savory Bacon and Gruyere Omelet	7
Savory Chicken Burgers	19
Savory Crab-Filled Mushrooms	60
Savory Dijon Beef Burger	35

Savory Onion, Pepper, and Mushroom Frittata	6
Savory Sausage Grill Medley	35
Savory Shrimp Skewers	26
Savory Steak and Mushroom with Balsamic Glaze	5
Seared Calamari with Herb Mustard Sauce	23
Seared Mahi-Mahi with Light Seasoning	27
Seared Salmon Kebabs with Seasoned Rub	29
Seared Scallops with Zesty Lemony Salsa Verde	27
Seared Scallops Wrapped in Crispy Bacon	31
Seared Sea Scallops with Corn Medley	23
Seared Shrimp in Velvety Shrimp Butter	31
Simple and Tender Sirloin Steaks	35
Sizzling Chicken Fajitas	14
Slow Roasted Shawarma	16
Slow-Cooked Texas Beef Brisket	34
Smashed Patty Burgers	39
Smoked Chicken in Maple Flavor	17
Smoked Healthy Cabbage	52
Smoked Jalapeño Poppers	51
Smoked Pickled Green Beans	56
Smoked Tomato and Mozzarella Dip	56
Smoked Whole Turkey	20
Speedy Marinade Skirt Steak	39
Spiced Jumbo Shrimp Skewers	25
Spiced Lamb Burger	44
Spiced Mexican Beef Salad	33
Spiced Pork Tenderloin with Harissa Cream Sauce	38
Spicy Mexican Scramble	10
Squid in Citrus Soy Marinade	28
Sticky Caramel Smoked Onion	51
Stir Fry Bok Choy	53
Stuffed Beef Rolls with Buttered Noodles	36
Sweet and Savory Pineapple Bacon Chops	33
Sweet Chili Lime Chicken	19

T

Tarragon Chicken Tenders	18
Tender Buttermilk Pork Roast	39
Tender Chicken Bacon Artichoke Delight	9
Tender Ham and Swiss Delight	4

Tex-Mex Turkey Burgers	49
Timeless Classic French Toast	9
Timeless Steak and Eggs	7
Tomatoes with Parmesan Cheese	62
Traditional Buttermilk Pancakes	8
Triple-Decker Monte Cristo Sandwich	45
Trout with a Touch of Rosemary	28
Turkey And Melted Brie Sandwich With Green Chiles	46
Turkey Burger	46
Turkey Legs	21
Turkey Pesto Panini	20
Tuscan-Style Grilled Shrimp	26
Tzatziki Lamb Burgers	48

U

Ultimate Grilled Cheese	44
Uncomplicated French Crepes	10

V

Vegetable Sandwich	55
Veggie Pesto Flatbread	44
Vietnamese Ground Pork Banh Mi	41

W

Warm Grilled Cinnamon Toast with Berries and Whipped Cream	6
White Chocolate Bread Pudding	65
White Wine and Parsley Marinated Trout	24

Y

Yucatan-Spiced Pork on the Griddle	39

Z

Zesty Lemon and Garlic Scallops	28